ANCIENT HISTORY ATLAS

ANCIENT HISTORY ATLAS

MICHAEL GRANT

Cartography by ARTHUR BANKS

The Macmillan Company, New York, New York

The Macmillan Company
866 Third Avenue, New York, N.Y. 10022
Collier-Macmillan Canada Ltd., Toronto, Ontario

Ancient History Atlas was first published in Great Britain in 1971 by Weidenfeld and Nicolson, London.

Library of Congress Catalog Card Number: 73-654430

First American Edition 1972

Second Printing 1973

Printed in the United States of America

Preface

This is, in the first place, an atlas of the classical world – the ancient Greek
and Roman world, which needs to be understood if we are to understand
the world of today. To say that such an atlas could ever be a substitute for
a historical survey would be an exaggeration. Nevertheless, geography is
such a vital, indeed predominant, factor in ancient history – and such a
difficult factor because of all the changes of names[1] – that the whole course
of events often seems to mean practically nothing without maps, and without
a lot of them, carefully devised.

Older classical atlases, apart from a varying degree of emphasis on physical
aspects, tended to concentrate on political themes, and it is true enough that
these stand in great need of maps. But the present volume attempts to cast
the net wider, and to introduce economic, cultural, religious and other topics
as well. There are also a number of town plans.

Modern research in archaeology and other fields has shown that the
classical world cannot be grasped without some appreciation of what went
before it. I have consequently started this book with a number of maps
illustrating the Mediterranean world during the second millennium BC, and
particularly during the period from 1700 BC onwards, when the international
scene had already assumed a well-defined and complex appearance; and the
story is carried onwards to offer brief illustrations of the Old Testament. At
the other end of the story, the traditional terminal date of the ancient world,
the year AD 476 when the last western emperor ceased to reign, is again not
a very meaningful landmark, so I have carried on the tale until the reign of
Justinian in the following century.

It will be clear enough what a very great deal is owed to the talent of
Mr Arthur Banks for transcribing the written and spoken word into
cartographic form. I am also most grateful to Mr Julian Shuckburgh for all
the assistance he has rendered on behalf of the publishers, and I want to
thank Miss Jane Dorner for assistance with the index. Finally, I have to
acknowledge a substantial debt to existing classical atlases, German and
English. And I must single out, for a special word of gratitude, the *Atlas of
the Classical World* edited by A. A. M. van der Heyden and H. H. Scullard
for Messrs Nelson, and *Westermanns Grosser Atlas zur Weltgeschichte*
(Westermann, Braunschweig). They have both given me ideas and material
for a number of maps.

MICHAEL GRANT
Gattaiola

1971

[1] Modern names are given after the ancient in the Index.

List of Maps

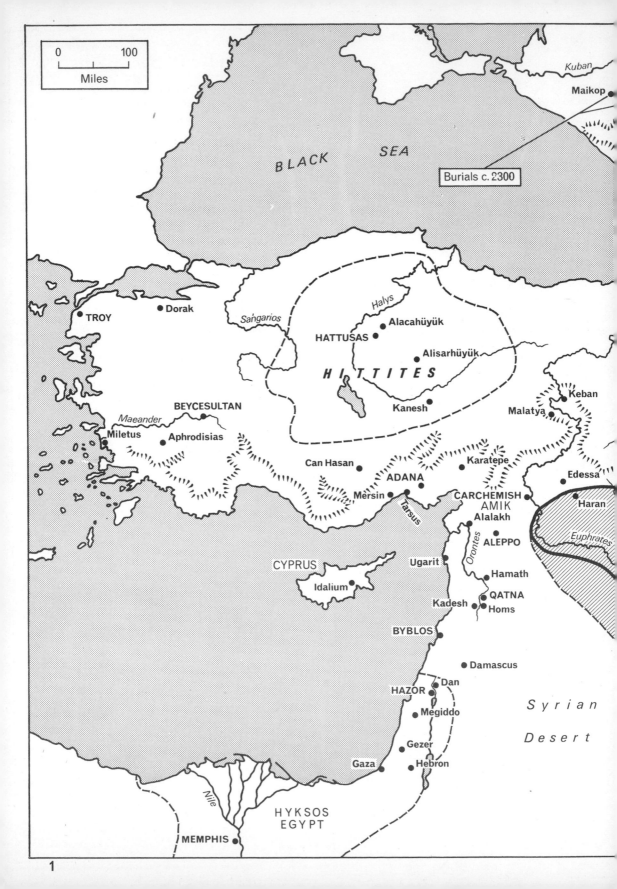

Scale: 0 — 100 Miles

Kuban

Maikop

BLACK SEA

Burials c. 2300

TROY ● Dorak

Sangarios

Halys

HATTUSAS ● Alacahüyük

Alisarhüyük ●

H I T T I T E S

Kanesh ●

Keban

Malatya

BEYCESULTAN

Maeander

Miletus ● Aphrodisias ●

Can Hasan ●

Karatepe ●

Edessa ●

ADANA

Mersin ● CARCHEMISH

Tarsus

AMIK

Alalakh

Haran ●

Euphrates

ALEPPO ●

CYPRUS

Idalium ● Ugarit ●

Orontes

Hamath ●

QATNA ●

Kadesh ● Homs ●

BYBLOS ●

● Damascus

Dan ●

HAZOR ●

Megiddo ●

S y r i a n

Gezer ●

D e s e r t

Gaza ● Hebron ●

Nile

HYKSOS
EGYPT

MEMPHIS ●

1

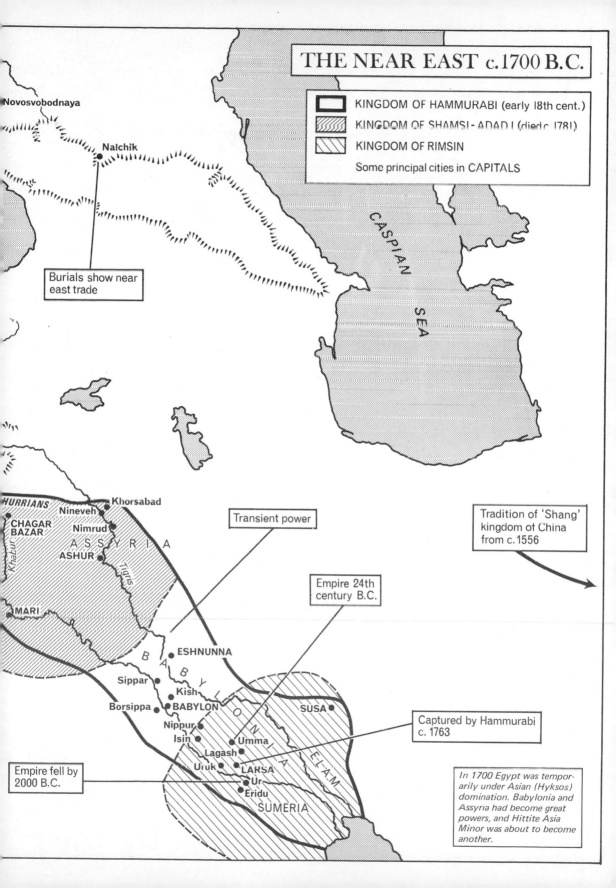

THE NEAR EAST c.1700 B.C.

☐ KINGDOM OF HAMMURABI (early 18th cent.)

▨ KINGDOM OF SHAMSI-ADAD I (died c.1781)

▧ KINGDOM OF RIMSIN

Some principal cities in CAPITALS

Novosvobodnaya

Nalchik

Burials show near east trade

CASPIAN SEA

HURRIANS

CHAGAR BAZAR

Khorsabad

Nineveh

Nimrud

ASSYRIA

ASHUR

Khabur

Tigris

MARI

Transient power

Tradition of 'Shang' kingdom of China from c.1556

Empire 24th century B.C.

BABYLONIA

ESHNUNNA

Sippar

Kish

Borsippa

BABYLON

Nippur

Isin

Umma

Lagash

Uruk

LARSA

Ur

Eridu

SUMERIA

SUSA

ELAM

Captured by Hammurabi c.1763

Empire fell by 2000 B.C.

In 1700 Egypt was temporarily under Asian (Hyksos) domination. Babylonia and Assyria had become great powers, and Hittite Asia Minor was about to become another.

THE NEAR EAST c. 1500–1400 B.C.

PLACE NAMES IN CAPITALS Capital cities

Egypt was now at the height of its power. In the 14th century, Mitanni (the Hurrians) succumbed to the Hittites.

Chinese civilisation with capital Anyang (Honan) c. 1400–1300

Connection with Near East broken after 1500

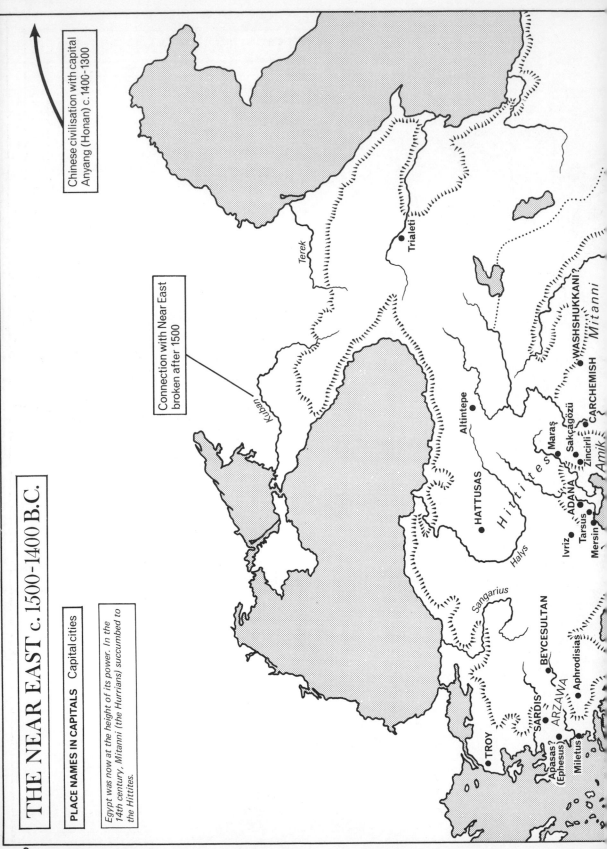

Terek

Kuban

Trialeti

Altintepe

HATTUSAS

Hittites

WASHSHUKKANI?

CARCHEMISH

Mitanni

Maraş

Sakçagözü

Zincirli

Amik

ADANA

Ivriz

Tarsus

Mersin

Halys

Sangarius

BEYCESULTAN

Aphrodisias

TROY

SARDIS

ARZAWA

Apasas? (Ephesus)

Miletus

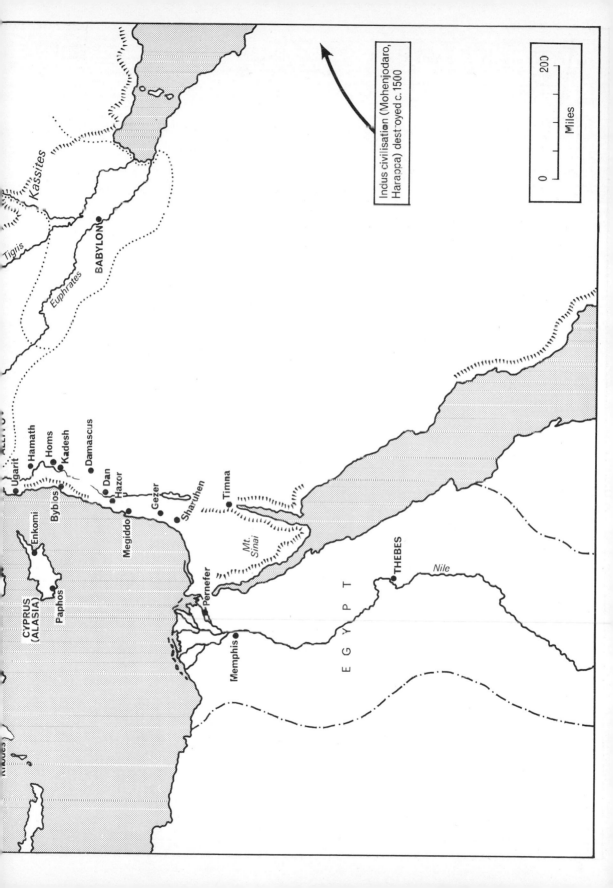

Indus civilisation (Mohenjodaro, Harappa) destroyed c.1500

200

Miles

0

Kassites

Tigris

Euphrates

BABYLON

ALEPPO

Ugarit
Hamath
Homs
Kadesh
Damascus

Byblos
Dan
Hazor

Enkomi
Gezer
Sharuhen
Timna

Paphos
Megiddo

CYPRUS
(ALASIA)

Mt.
Sinai

Pernefer

THEBES

Nile

E G Y P T

Memphis

RHODES

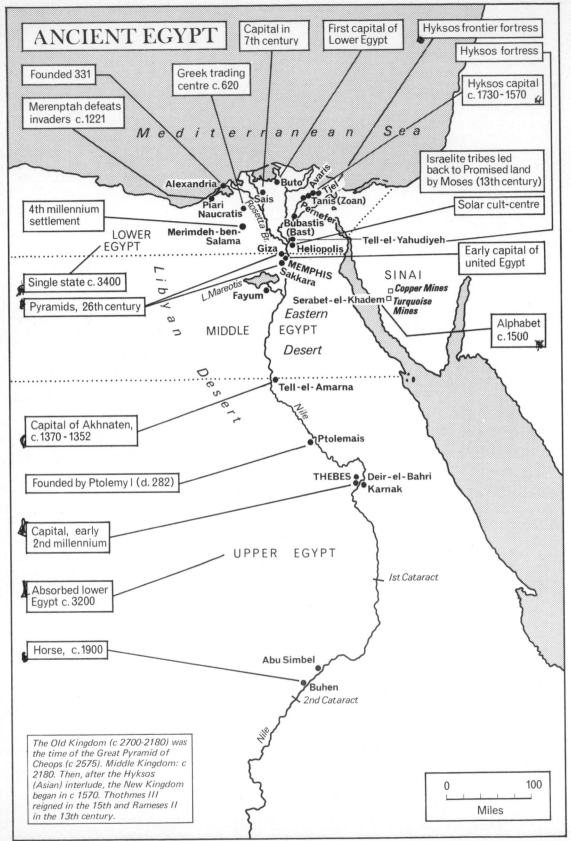

ANCIENT EGYPT

Founded 331

Merenptah defeats invaders c.1221

Greek trading centre c. 620

Capital in 7th century

First capital of Lower Egypt

Hyksos frontier fortress

Hyksos fortress

Hyksos capital c.1730 - 1570

Israelite tribes led back to Promised land by Moses (13th century)

Mediterranean Sea

4th millennium settlement

Alexandria

Buto

Avaris

Tiel

Tanis (Zoan)

Solar cult-centre

Piari Naucratis

Sais

Rosetta Br.

Pernefer

LOWER EGYPT

Merimdeh-ben-Salama

Bubastis (Bast)

Single state c. 3400

Pyramids, 26th century

Libyan

Giza

Heliopolis

Tell-el-Yahudiyeh

Early capital of united Egypt

MEMPHIS

Sakkara

SINAI

□ *Copper Mines*

L.Mareotis

Fayum

MIDDLE

Eastern

Serabet-el-Khadem □ *Turquoise Mines*

EGYPT

Alphabet c.1500

Desert

Desert

Tell-el-Amarna

Capital of Akhnaten, c.1370 - 1352

Nile

Ptolemais

Founded by Ptolemy I (d. 282)

THEBES **Deir-el-Bahri**

Karnak

Capital, early 2nd millennium

UPPER EGYPT

1st Cataract

Absorbed lower Egypt c.3200

Horse, c.1900

Abu Simbel

Buhen

2nd Cataract

Nile

The Old Kingdom (c 2700-2180) was the time of the Great Pyramid of Cheops (c 2575). Middle Kingdom: c 2180. Then, after the Hyksos (Asian) interlude, the New Kingdom began in c 1570. Thothmes III reigned in the 15th and Rameses II in the 13th century.

0   100

Miles

3

MINOAN CRETE AND THE AEGEAN

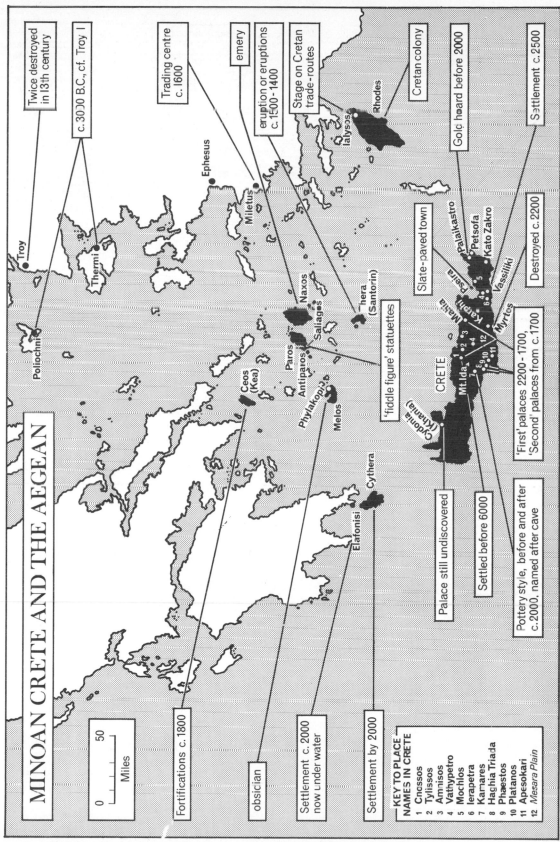

Twice destroyed in 13th century

c. 3000 B.C., cf. Troy I

Trading centre c. 1600

emery

eruption or eruptions c. 1500 - 1400

Stage on Cretan trade-routes

Cretan colony

Gold hoard before 2000

Settlement c. 2500

Destroyed c. 2200

Slate-paved town

'First' palaces 2200 - 1700, 'Second' palaces from c. 1700

Pottery style, before and after c. 2000, named after cave

Settled before 6000

Palace still undiscovered

Settlement by 2000

Settlement c. 2000 now under water

obsidian

Fortifications c. 1800

'fiddle figure' statuettes

Ephesus

Miletus

Troy

Thermi

Poliochni

Naxos

Saliagos

Paros

Antiparos

Ceos (Kea)

Phylakopi

Melos

Elafonisi

Cythera

Thera (Santorin)

Rhodes

Ialysos

CRETE

Mt. Ida

Cnossos

Cydonia (Khania)

Mastia

Kaphti

Psaira

Palaikastro

Petsofa

Kato Zakro

Vassiliki

Myrtos

0   50

Miles

KEY TO PLACE NAMES IN CRETE

1 Cnossos
2 Tylissos
3 Amnisos
4 Vathypetro
5 Mochlos
6 Ierapetra
7 Karnares
8 Hachia Triada
9 Phaestos
10 Platanos
11 Apesokari
12 *Mesara Plain*

4

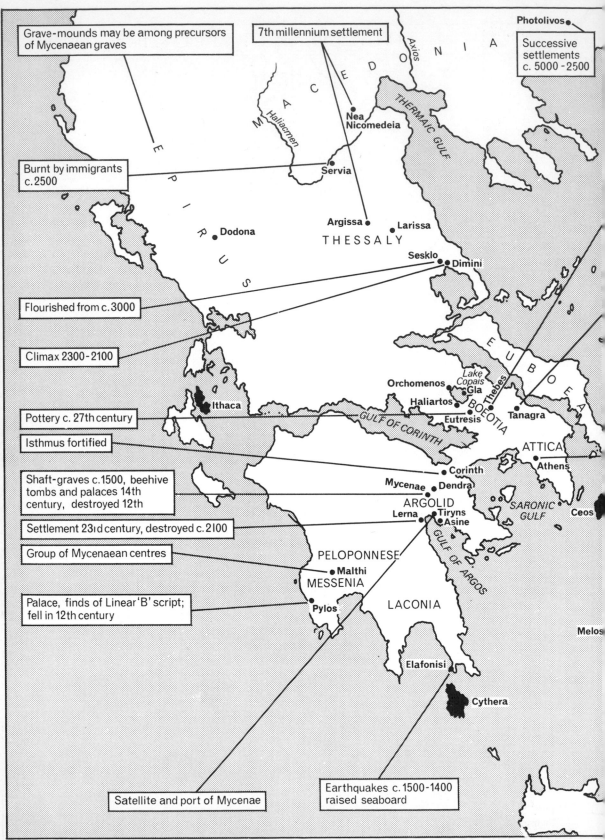

Grave-mounds may be among precursors of Mycenaean graves

7th millennium settlement

Successive settlements c. 5000 - 2500

Photolivos•

Axios

M A C E D O N I A

THERMAIC GULF

Haliacmen

Nea Nicomedeia•

Burnt by immigrants c. 2500

Servia•

E P I R U S

Dodona•

Argissa•   Larissa•

THESSALY

Sesklo• •Dimini

Flourished from c. 3000

Climax 2300 - 2100

E U B O E A

Lake Copais

Orchomenos• Gla• Thebes•

•Ithaca

Haliartos•   BOEOTIA

Pottery c. 27th century

Eutresis•   Tanagra•

Isthmus fortified

GULF OF CORINTH

ATTICA

Athens•

Corinth•

Shaft-graves c.1500, beehive tombs and palaces 14th century, destroyed 12th

Mycenae• •Dendra

ARGOLID

SARONIC GULF

Ceos•

Lerna• Tiryns•

Settlement 23rd century, destroyed c. 2100

•Asine

Group of Mycenaean centres

PELOPONNESE

GULF OF ARGOS

•Malthi

Palace, finds of Linear 'B' script; fell in 12th century

MESSENIA

LACONIA

Pylos•

Melos

Elafonisi•

Cythera•

Satellite and port of Mycenae

Earthquakes c.1500-1400 raised seaboard

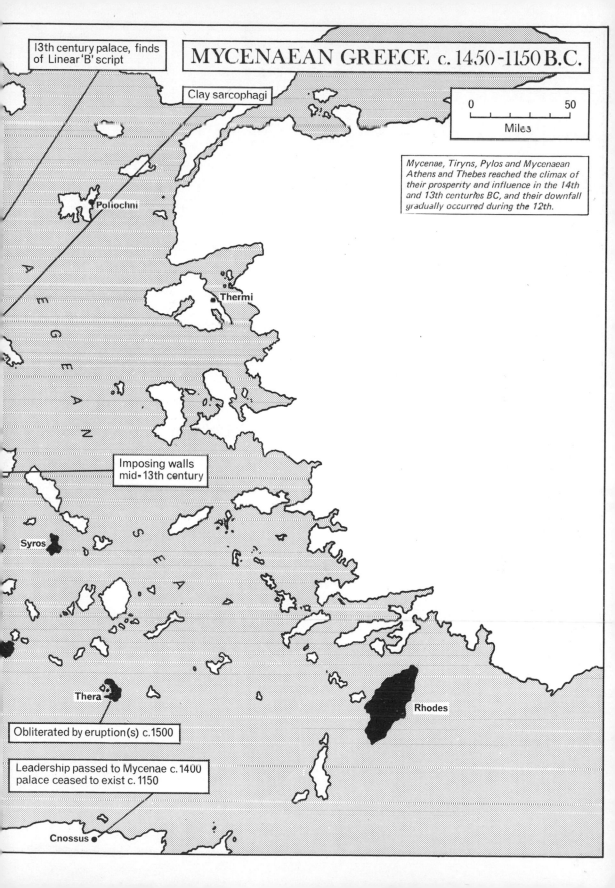

MYCENAEAN GREECE c. 1450-1150 B.C.

13th century palace, finds of Linear 'B' script

Clay sarcophagi

0   50

Miles

Mycenae, Tiryns, Pylos and Mycenaean Athens and Thebes reached the climax of their prosperity and influence in the 14th and 13th centuries BC, and their downfall gradually occurred during the 12th.

A E G E A N

Poliochni

Thermi

Imposing walls mid-13th century

S E A

Syros

Thera

Rhodes

Obliterated by eruption(s) c.1500

Leadership passed to Mycenae c.1400 palace ceased to exist c.1150

Cnossus

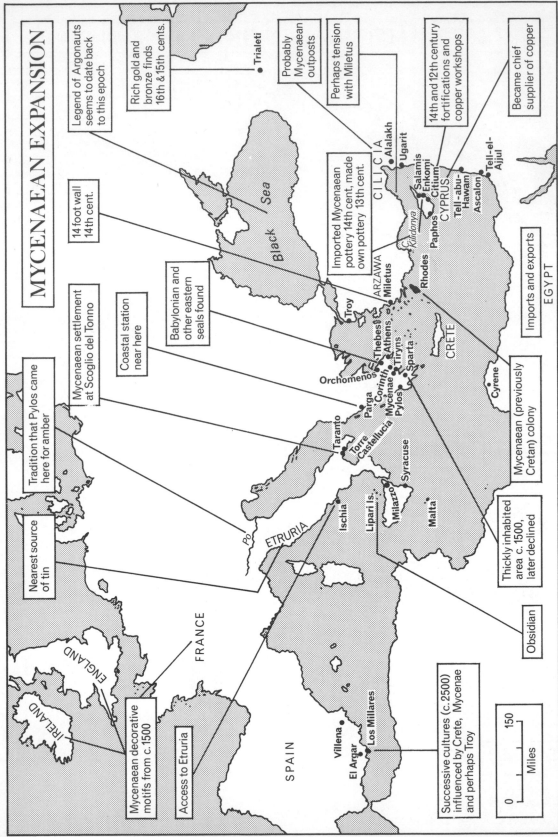

MYCENAEAN EXPANSION

Legend of Argonauts seems to date back to this epoch

Rich gold and bronze finds 16th & 15th cents.

Probably Mycenaean outposts

Perhaps tension with Miletus

14th and 12th century fortifications and copper workshops

Became chief supplier of copper

14 foot wall 14th cent.

Imported Mycenaean pottery 14th cent, made own pottery 13th cent.

Mycenaean settlement at Scoglio del Tonno

Coastal station near here

Babylonian and other eastern seals found

Tradition that Pylos came here for amber

Nearest source of tin

Mycenaean decorative motifs from c. 1500

Access to Etruria

Imports and exports

Mycenaean (previously Cretan) colony

Thickly inhabited area c. 1500, later declined

Obsidian

Successive cultures (c. 2500) influenced by Crete, Mycenae and perhaps Troy

Trialeti

Black Sea

CILICIA
Alalakh
Ugarit
Salamis
Enkomi
Citium?
CYPRUS
Paphos
Tell-abu-Hawam
Ascalon
Tell-el-Ajjul

ARZAWA
Miletus
C. Kilidonya
Rhodes

Troy

Thebes
Athens
Corinth
Tiryns
Orchomenos
Mycenae
Sparta
Pylos
Parga

CRETE

Cyrene

EGYPT

Taranto
Torre Castellucia

Syracuse

Ischia
Lipari Is.
Milazzo
Malta

Po
ETRURIA

FRANCE

ENGLAND

IRELAND

SPAIN

Villena
El Argar
Los Millares

0   150
Miles

6

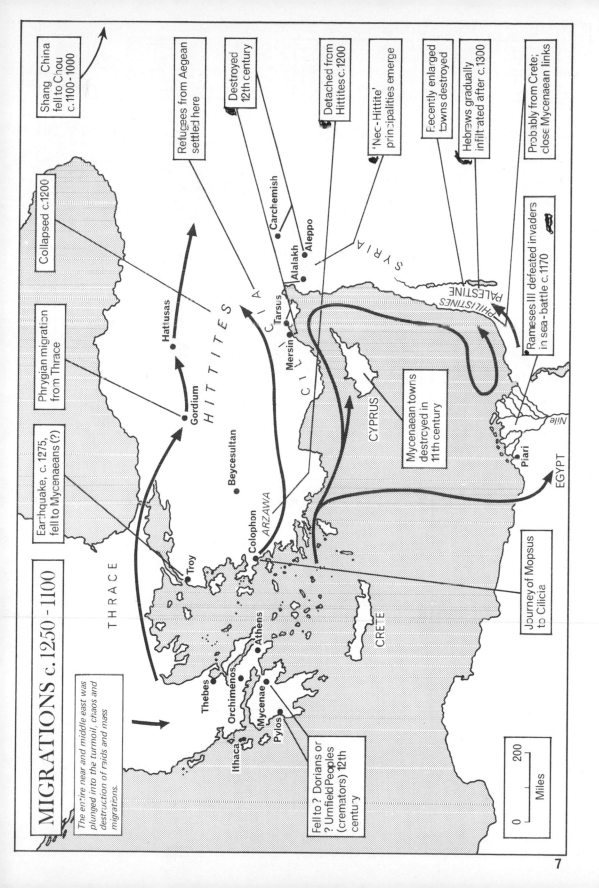

MIGRATIONS c. 1250 - 1100

The entire near and middle east was plunged into the turmoil, chaos and destruction of raids and mass migrations.

Shang China fell to Chou c. 1100-1000

Refugees from Aegean settle here

Destroyed 12th century

Detached from Hittites c. 1200

'Neo-Hittite' principalities emerge

Recently enlarged towns destroyed

Hebrews gradually infiltrated after c.1300

Probably from Crete; close Mycenaean links

Collapsed c.1200

Phrygian migration from Thrace

Earthquake, c. 1275, fell to Mycenaeans (?)

Rameses III defeated invaders in sea-battle c. 1170

Mycenaean towns destroyed in 11th century

Journey of Mopsus to Cilicia

Fell to ? Dorians or ? Urnfield Peoples (cremators) 12th century

THRACE

HITTITES

ARZAWA

CILICIA

SYRIA

PALESTINE

PHILISTINES

CYPRUS

CRETE

EGYPT

Nile

Carchemish

Aleppo

Alalakh

Tarsus

Mersin

Hattusas

Gordium

Beycesultan

Colophon

Troy

Thebes

Orchimenos

Athens

Mycenae

Pylos

Ithaca

Piari

0   200

Miles

7

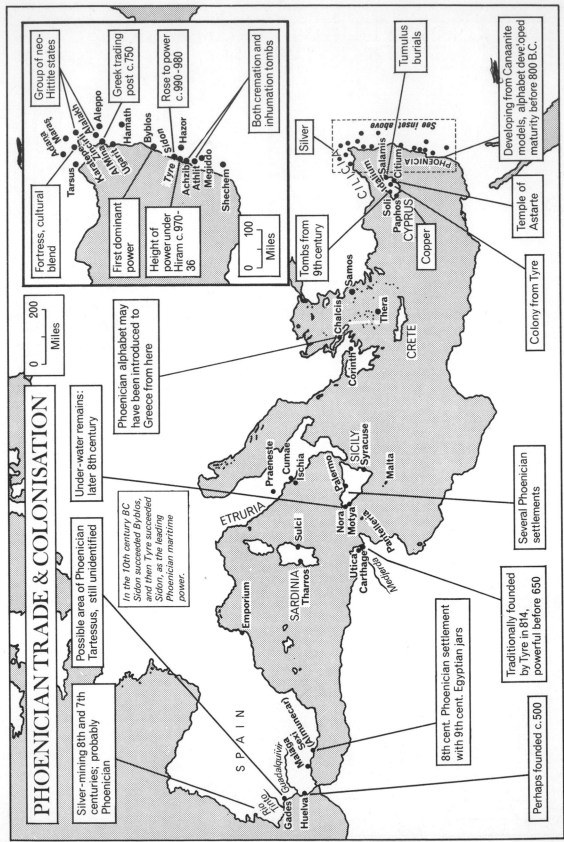

PHOENICIAN TRADE & COLONISATION

Silver-mining 8th and 7th centuries; probably Phoenician

Possible area of Phoenician Tartessus, still unidentified

Under-water remains: later 8th century

Phoenician alphabet may have been introduced to Greece from here

In the 10th century BC Sidon succeeded Byblos, and then Tyre succeeded Sidon, as the leading Phoenician maritime power.

Several Phoenician settlements

Traditionally founded by Tyre in 814, powerful before 650

8th cent. Phoenician settlement with 9th cent. Egyptian jars

Perhaps founded c.500

0   200
Miles

SPAIN
Rio Tinto
Guadalquivir
Gades
Huelva
Malaga
Sexi (Almuñecar)
EMPORIUM
SARDINIA
Tharros
Sulci
Nora
Motya
Panormus
Utica
Carthage
Medjerda
ETRURIA
Praeneste
Cumae
Ischia
Palermo
SICILY
Syracuse
Malta
Chalcis
Samos
Corinth
Thera
CRETE

Inset (top)

Group of neo-Hittite states

Greek trading post c.750

Rose to power c.990-980

Both cremation and inhumation tombs

Tumulus burials

Developing from Canaanite models, alphabet dev'oped maturity before 800 B.C.

Fortress, cultural blend

First dominant power

Height of power under Hiram c.970-36

Tombs from 9th century

Silver

Copper

Colony from Tyre

Temple of Astarte

Adana Maraş
Tarsus
Karatepe Alalakh
Al Mina Ugarit
Aleppo
Hamath
Byblos
Sidon
Tyre Hazor
Achzib
Athlit
Megiddo
Shechem

0   100
Miles

CILICIA
Soli Salamis
Paphos Citium
CYPRUS
PHOENICIA
See inset above

8

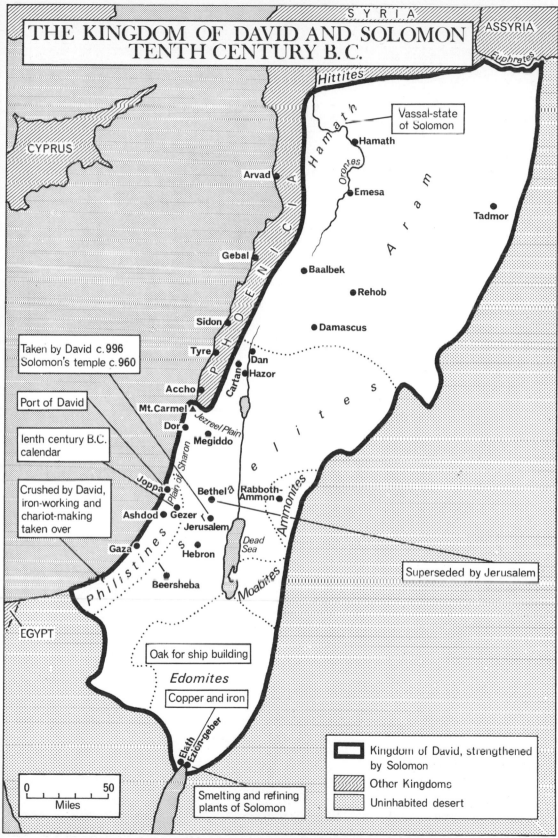

THE KINGDOM OF DAVID AND SOLOMON TENTH CENTURY B.C.

SYRIA

ASSYRIA

Euphrates

Hittites

Hamath

Vassal-state of Solomon

Hamath

Orontes

Arvad

Emesa

Tadmor

CYPRUS

Gebal

Baalbek

Rehob

A r a m

Sidon

Damascus

Tyre

Taken by David c.996
Solomon's temple c.960

Dan

Cartan

Hazor

Accho

Mt. Carmel

Jezreel Plain

I s r a e l i t e s

Port of David

Dor

Megiddo

Tenth century B.C.
calendar

Plain of Sharon

Joppa

Bethel

Rabboth-
Ammon

Crushed by David,
iron-working and
chariot-making
taken over

Ashdod

Gezer

Jerusalem

Ammonites

Gaza

Hebron

Dead
Sea

Superseded by Jerusalem

Beersheba

Moabites

EGYPT

P h i l i s t i n e s

Oak for ship building

Edomites

Copper and iron

Elath
Ezion-geber

Kingdom of David, strengthened
by Solomon

Other Kingdoms

Uninhabited desert

Smelting and refining
plants of Solomon

0 ————— 50
Miles

9

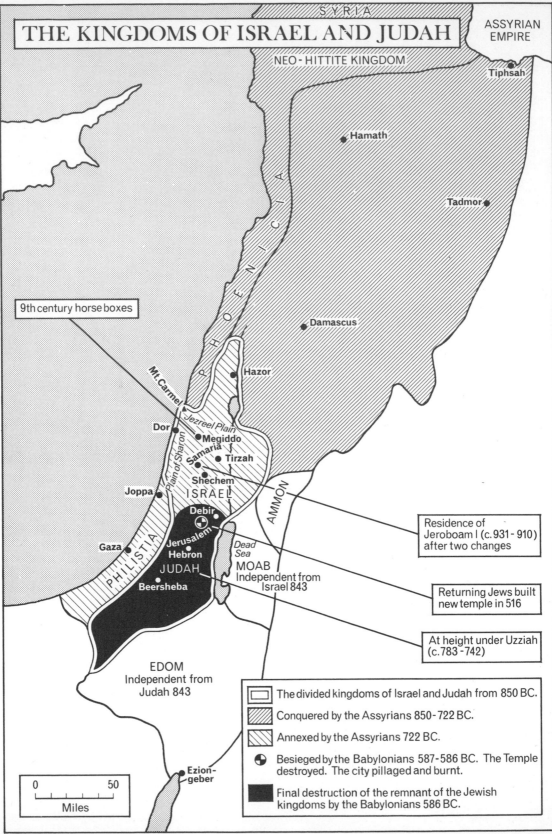

THE KINGDOMS OF ISRAEL AND JUDAH

SYRIA

ASSYRIAN EMPIRE

NEO-HITTITE KINGDOM

Tiphsah

Hamath

Tadmor

P H O E N I C I A

9th century horse boxes

Mt. Carmel

Jezreel Plain

Damascus

Hazor

Dor

Megiddo

Plain of Sharon

Samaria

Tirzah

Shechem

Joppa

ISRAEL

AMMON

Debir

Jerusalem

Hebron

Gaza

PHILISTIA

Dead Sea

Beersheba

JUDAH

MOAB
Independent from
Israel 843

Residence of
Jeroboam I (c. 931 - 910)
after two changes

Returning Jews built
new temple in 516

At height under Uzziah
(c. 783 - 742)

EDOM
Independent from
Judah 843

Ezion-geber

0   50
Miles

☐ The divided kingdoms of Israel and Judah from 850 BC.

▨ Conquered by the Assyrians 850 - 722 BC.

▨ Annexed by the Assyrians 722 BC.

⊕ Besieged by the Babylonians 587 - 586 BC. The Temple destroyed. The city pillaged and burnt.

■ Final destruction of the remnant of the Jewish kingdoms by the Babylonians 586 BC.

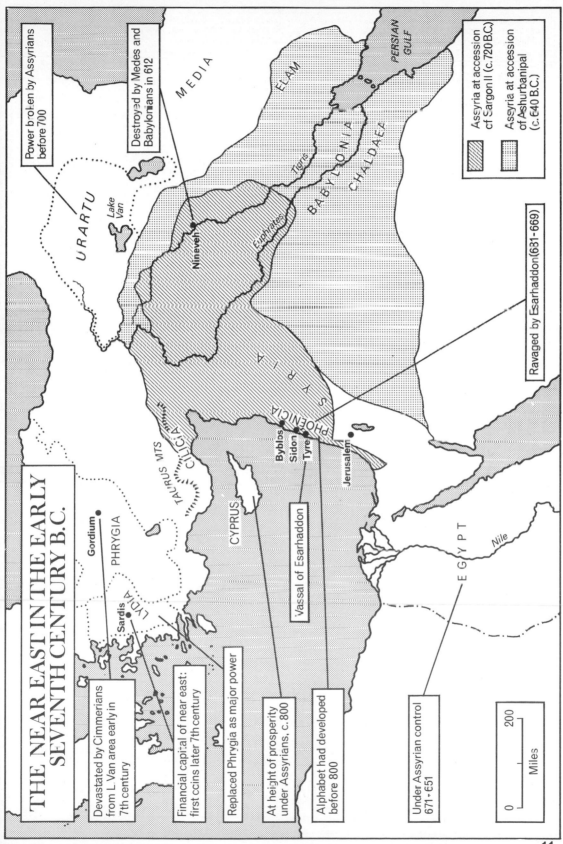

THE NEAR EAST IN THE EARLY SEVENTH CENTURY B.C.

Devastated by Cimmerians from L. Van area early in 7th century

Financial capital of near east: first coins later 7th century

Replaced Phrygia as major power

At height of prosperity under Assyrians, c. 800

Alphabet had developed before 800

Under Assyrian control 671-651

Power broken by Assyrians before 700

Destroyed by Medes and Babylonians in 612

Assyria at accession of Sargon II (c. 720 B.C.)

Assyria at accession of Ashurbanipal (c. 640 B.C.)

Ravaged by Esarhaddon (681-669)

Vassal of Esarhaddon

URARTU

Lake Van

MEDIA

ELAM

Tigris

BABYLONIA

CHALDAEA

PERSIAN GULF

Nineveh

Euphrates

SYRIA

TAURUS MTS

CILICIA

PHOENICIA

Byblos

Sidon

Tyre

Jerusalem

CYPRUS

PHRYGIA

Gordium

LYDIA

Sardis

EGYPT

Nile

0   200

Miles

11

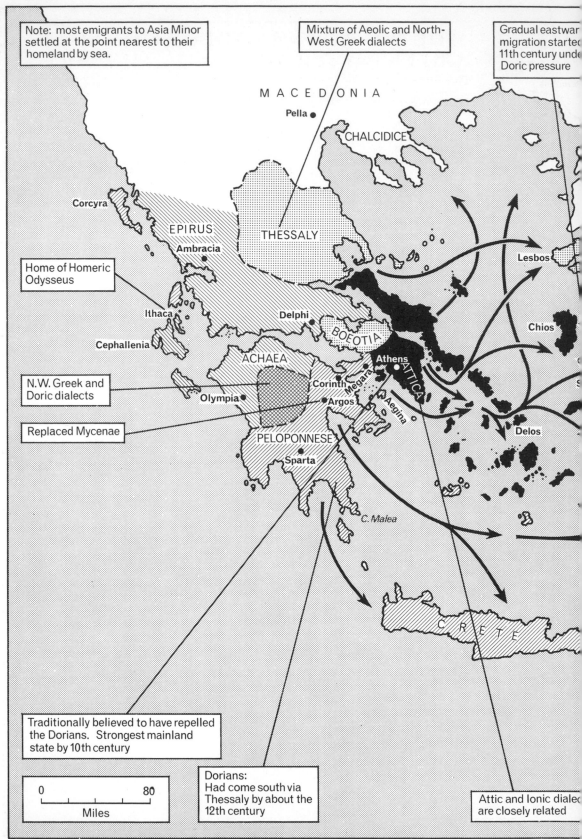

Note: most emigrants to Asia Minor settled at the point nearest to their homeland by sea.

Mixture of Aeolic and North-West Greek dialects

Gradual eastward migration started 11th century under Doric pressure

M A C E D O N I A

Pella

CHALCIDICE

Corcyra

EPIRUS

THESSALY

Ambracia

Lesbos

Home of Homeric Odysseus

Ithaca

Delphi

Chios

Cephallenia

BOEOTIA

ACHAEA

Athens

N.W. Greek and Doric dialects

Corinth

Megara

ATTICA

Olympia

Argos

Aegina

Delos

Replaced Mycenae

PELOPONNESE

Sparta

C. Malea

CRETE

Traditionally believed to have repelled the Dorians. Strongest mainland state by 10th century

0   80

Miles

Dorians: Had come south via Thessaly by about the 12th century

Attic and Ionic dialect are closely related

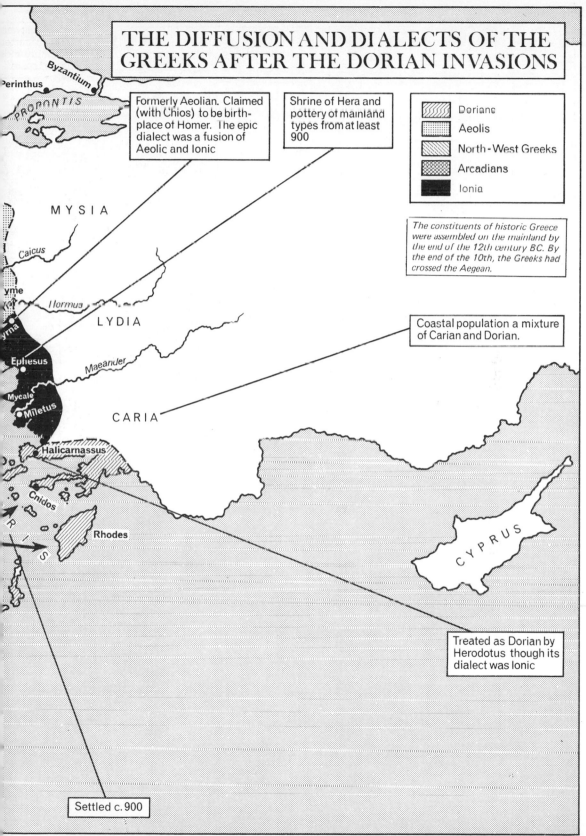

THE DIFFUSION AND DIALECTS OF THE GREEKS AFTER THE DORIAN INVASIONS

Formerly Aeolian. Claimed (with Chios) to be birth-place of Homer. The epic dialect was a fusion of Aeolic and Ionic

Shrine of Hera and pottery of mainland types from at least 900

▨	Dorians
▦	Aeolis
▨	North-West Greeks
▧	Arcadians
■	Ionia

The constituents of historic Greece were assembled on the mainland by the end of the 12th century BC. By the end of the 10th, the Greeks had crossed the Aegean.

Coastal population a mixture of Carian and Dorian.

Treated as Dorian by Herodotus though its dialect was Ionic

Settled c. 900

Byzantium
Perinthus
PROPONTIS

MYSIA

Caicus

yme

Hormus

LYDIA

rna

Ephesus

Maeander

Mycale

Miletus

CARIA

Halicarnassus

Cnidos

Rhodes

CYPRUS

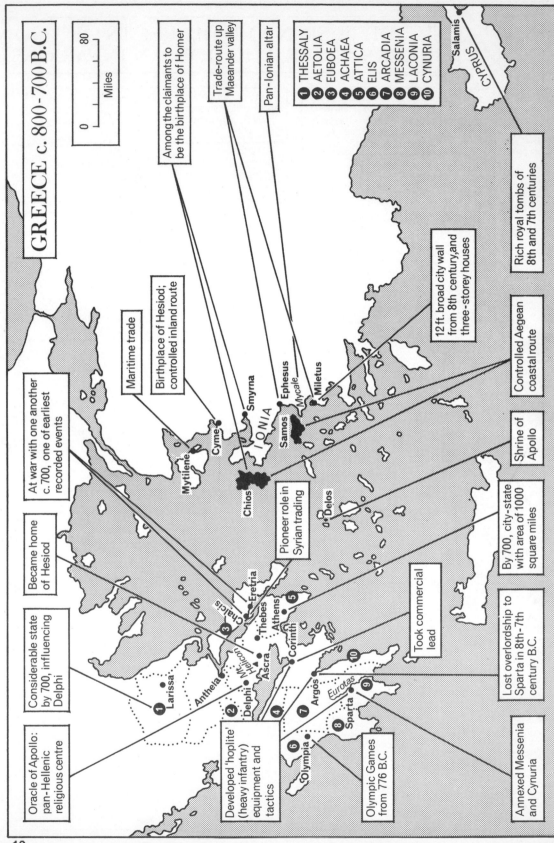

GREECE c. 800-700 B.C.

Miles 0 — 80

1 THESSALY
2 AETOLIA
3 EUBOEA
4 ACHAEA
5 ATTICA
6 ELIS
7 ARCADIA
8 MESSENIA
9 LACONIA
10 CYNURIA

Among the claimants to be the birthplace of Homer

Trade-route up Maeander valley

Pan-Ionian altar

Maritime trade

Birthplace of Hesiod; controlled inland route

At war with one another c.700, one of earliest recorded events

Became home of Hesiod

Considerable state by 700, influencing Delphi

Oracle of Apollo: pan-Hellenic religious centre

Developed 'hoplite' (heavy infantry) equipment and tactics

Olympic Games from 776 B.C.

Annexed Messenia and Cynuria

Took commercial lead

Lost overlordship to Sparta in 8th-7th century B.C.

By 700, city-state with area of 1000 square miles

Shrine of Apollo

Controlled Aegean coastal route

Rich royal tombs of 8th and 7th centuries

12 ft. broad city wall from 8th century, and three-storey houses

Pioneer role in Syrian trading

CYPRUS

Salamis

Smyrna

Ephesus

Mycale

Miletus

Samos

IONIA

Chios

Cyme

Mytilene

Delos

Eretria

Chalcis

Thebes

Athens

Corinth

Larissa

Anthela

Delphi

Mt. Helicon

Ascra

Argos

Eurotas

Sparta

Olympia

13

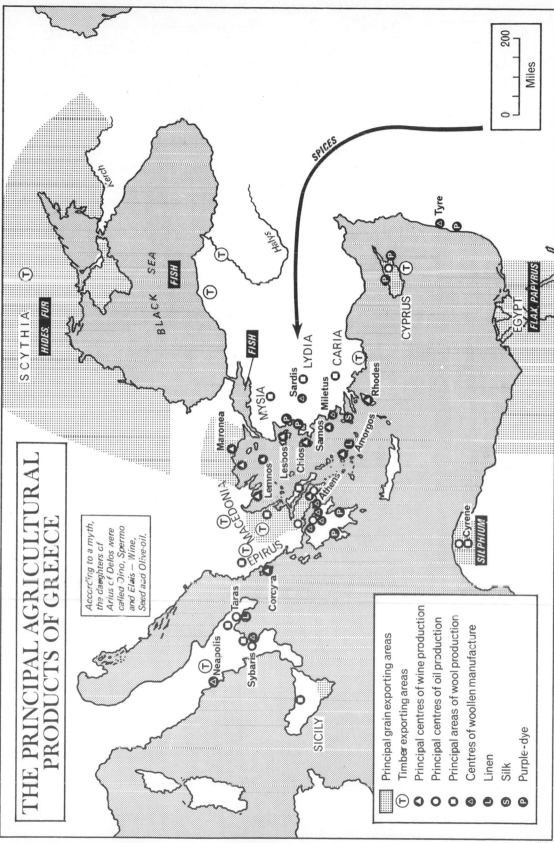

THE PRINCIPAL AGRICULTURAL PRODUCTS OF GREECE

According to a myth, the daughters of Arius of Delos were called Oino, Spermo and Elais — Wine, Seed and Olive-oil.

Legend:
- Principal grain exporting areas
- Timber exporting areas
- (T)
- Principal centres of wine production
- Principal centres of oil production
- Principal areas of wool production
- Centres of woollen manufacture
- (L) Linen
- (S) Silk
- (P) Purple-dye

Map labels: SCYTHIA, HIDES, FUR, BLACK SEA, FISH, Kerch, Halys, SPICES, Tyre, CYPRUS, EGYPT, FLAX, PAPYRUS, LYDIA, Sardis, CARIA, Miletus, Rhodes, MYSIA, Maronea, Lemnos, Lesbos, Chios, Samos, Amorgos, Athens, MACEDONIA, EPIRUS, Corcyra, Taras, Neapolis, Sybaris, SICILY, Cyrene, SILPHIUM

200 Miles

MEDITERRANEAN MOUNTAINS AND RIVERS

The rivers which flow down from these mountains are violent and erratic. Only the Nile, Tiber, Po, Ebro and Rhone are relatively stable; and even they are hazardous.

0 — 300
Miles

① Propontis
② River Caicus
③ River Hermus
④ River Cayster
⑤ River Maeander
⑥ River Peneus
⑦ River Sarus
⑧ River Pyramus

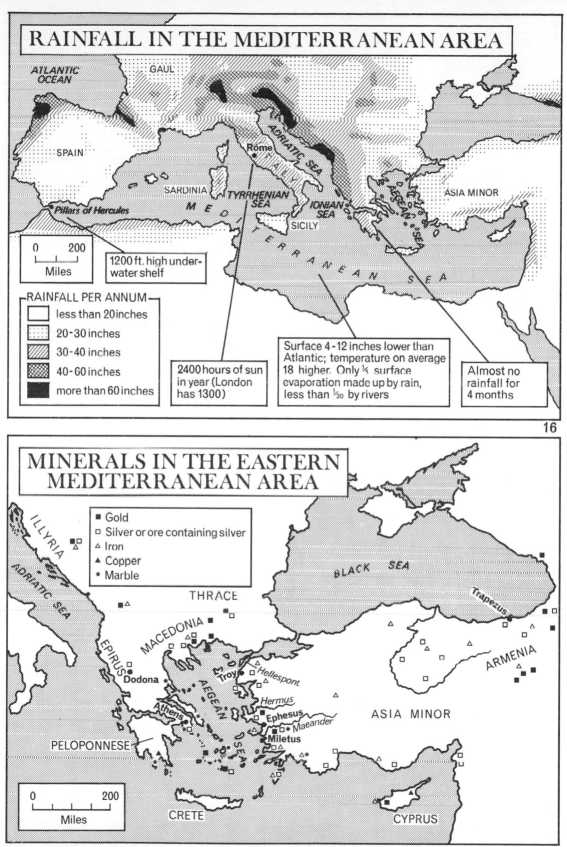

RAINFALL IN THE MEDITERRANEAN AREA

ATLANTIC OCEAN

GAUL

SPAIN

SARDINIA

Pillars of Hercules

Rome

ITALY

ADRIATIC SEA

TYRRHENIAN SEA

IONIAN SEA

SICILY

M E D I T E R R A N E A N   S E A

AEGEAN SEA

ASIA MINOR

0   200
Miles

1200 ft. high under-water shelf

RAINFALL PER ANNUM

	less than 20 inches
	20-30 inches
	30-40 inches
	40-60 inches
	more than 60 inches

2400 hours of sun in year (London has 1300)

Surface 4-12 inches lower than Atlantic; temperature on average 18 higher. Only ¼ surface evaporation made up by rain, less than ¹⁄₂₀ by rivers

Almost no rainfall for 4 months

MINERALS IN THE EASTERN MEDITERRANEAN AREA

■ Gold
□ Silver or ore containing silver
△ Iron
▲ Copper
* Marble

ILLYRIA

ADRIATIC SEA

BLACK SEA

THRACE

Trapezus

MACEDONIA

EPIRUS

Dodona

Troy

Hellespont

ARMENIA

Hermus

Athens

Ephesus

Maeander

ASIA MINOR

AEGEAN SEA

Miletus

PELOPONNESE

CRETE

CYPRUS

0   200
Miles

THE RELIGIOUS CENTRES OF GREECE

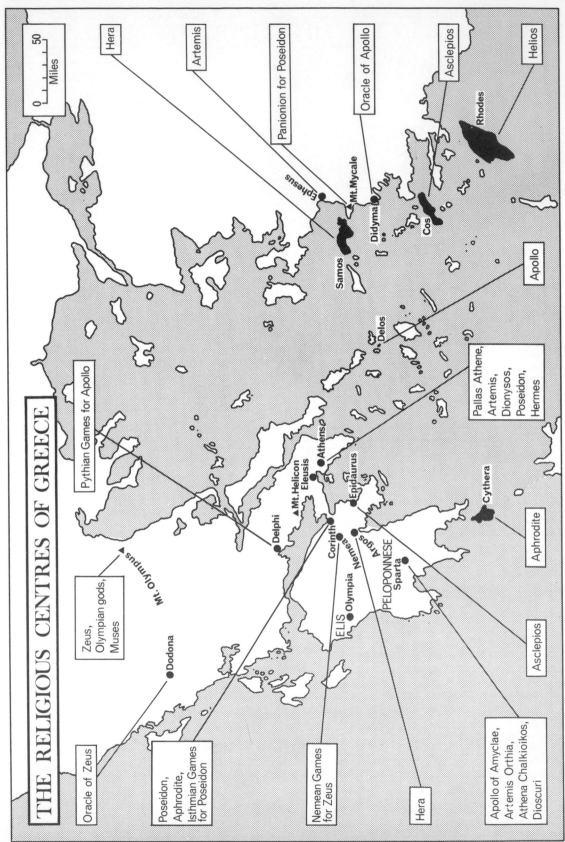

50 Miles

Hera

Artemis

Panionion for Poseidon

Oracle of Apollo

Asclepios

Helios

Rhodes

Ephesus

Mt. Mycale

Didyma

Cos

Samos

Apollo

Delos

Pallas Athene, Artemis, Dionysos, Poseidon, Hermes

Pythian Games for Apollo

Mt. Helicon

Eleusis

Athens

Epidaurus

Cythera

Aphrodite

Zeus, Olympian gods, Muses

Mt. Olympus

Delphi

Corinth

Nemea

Argos

PELOPONNESE

Sparta

Asclepios

Oracle of Zeus

Poseidon, Aphrodite, Isthmian Games for Poseidon

Dodona

ELIS

Olympia

Nemean Games for Zeus

Hera

Apollo of Amyclae, Artemis Orthia, Athena Chalkioikos, Dioscuri

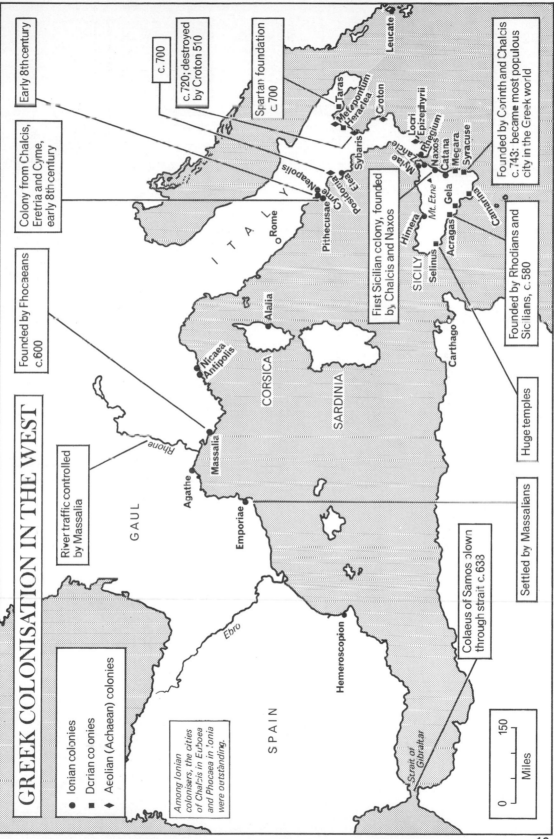

GREEK COLONISATION IN THE WEST

Legend:
- ● Ionian colonies
- ■ Dorian colonies
- ◆ Aeolian (Achaean) colonies

Among Ionian colonisers, the cities of Chalcis in Euboea and Phocaea in Ionia were outstanding.

Early 8th century

c. 700

c. 720; destroyed by Croton 510

Spartan foundation c. 700

Colony from Chalcis, Eretria and Cyme, early 8th century

Founded by Phocaeans c. 600

River traffic controlled by Massalia

First Sicilian colony, founded by Chalcis and Naxos

Founded by Corinth and Chalcis c. 743; became most populous city in the Greek world

Founded by Rhodians and Sicilians, c. 580

Huge temples

Settled by Massalians

Colaeus of Samos blown through strait c. 633

Place names:
Leucate, Taras, Metapontum, Heraclea, Croton, Locri Epizephyrii, Rhegium, Mylae, Zancle, Naxos, Catana, Megara, Syracuse, Sybaris, Elea, Posidonia, Cyme, Neapolis, Pithecusae, Rome, Himera, Mt. Etna, Gela, Acragas, Selinus, Camarina, SICILY

ITALY, GAUL, CORSICA, SARDINIA, SPAIN, Carthago

Alalia, Nicaea, Antipolis, Massalia, Agathe, Emporiae, Hemeroscopion, Strait of Gibraltar

Rhone, Ebro

Scale: 0 — 150 Miles

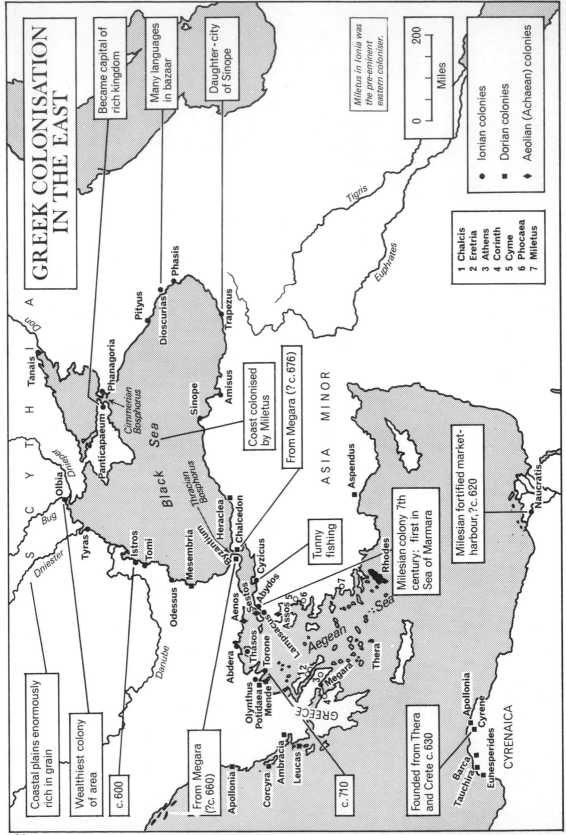

GREEK COLONISATION IN THE EAST

Miletus in Ionia was the pre-eminent eastern coloniser.

200

0

Miles

- ● Ionian colonies
- ■ Dorian colonies
- ◆ Aeolian (Achaean) colonies

1 Chalcis
2 Eretria
3 Athens
4 Corinth
5 Cyme
6 Phocaea
7 Miletus

Became capital of rich kingdom

Many languages in bazaar

Daughter-city of Sinope

Tigris

Euphrates

Don

SCYTHIA

Tanais I

Phanagoria

Panticapaeum

Cimmerian Bosphorus

Black Sea

Pityus

Dioscurias

Phasis

Sinope

Amisus

Trapezus

ASIA MINOR

Coast colonised by Miletus

From Megara (? c. 676)

Dnieper

Olbia

Bug

Tyras

Dniester

Istros

Tomi

Mesembria

Odessus

Thracian Bosphorus

Byzantium

Heraclea

Chalcedon

Cyzicus

Aspendus

Tunny fishing

Milesian colony 7th century: first in Sea of Marmara

Milesian fortified market-harbour, ? c. 620

Naucratis

Danube

Coastal plains enormously rich in grain

Wealthiest colony of area

c. 600

From Megara (? c. 660)

Aenos

Sestos

Abydos

Lampsacus

Assos 5

6

7

Rhodes

Aegean Sea

Abdera

Thasos

Torone

Olynthus

Potidaea

Mende

1 2

3

Megara

Thera

GREECE

Apollonia

Corcyra

Ambracia

Leucas

c. 710

Founded from Thera and Crete c. 630

Apollonia

Cyrene

Barca

Tauchira

Euesperides

CYRENAICA

20

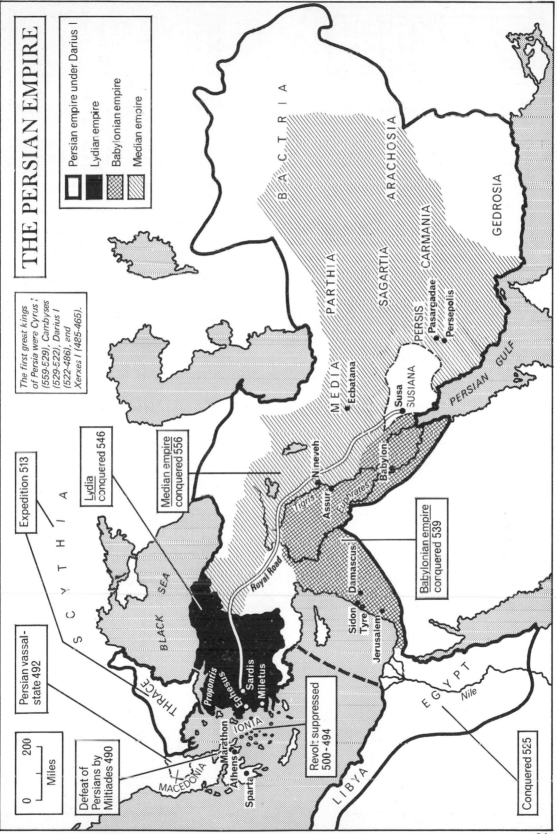

THE PERSIAN EMPIRE

Persian empire under Darius I
Lydian empire
Babylonian empire
Median empire

The first great kings of Persia were Cyrus I (559-529), Cambyses (529-522), Darius I (522-486), and Xerxes I (485-465).

Expedition 513

Lydia conquered 546

Median empire conquered 556

Persian vassal-state 492

Babylonian empire conquered 539

0   200
Miles

Defeat of Persians by Miltiades 490

Revolt: suppressed 500 - 494

Conquered 525

BACTRIA

ARACHOSIA

GEDROSIA

PARTHIA

SAGARTIA

CARMANIA

PERSIS
Pasargadae
Persepolis

MEDIA
Ecbatana

Susa
SUSIANA

PERSIAN GULF

Nineveh
Tigris
Assur
Euphrates
Babylon

Royal Road

SCYTHIA

BLACK SEA

THRACE

Propontis
Ephesus
Sardis
Miletus

Marathon
Athens
IONIA

MACEDONIA

Sparta

Damascus
Sidon
Tyre
Jerusalem

EGYPT
Nile

LIBYA

21

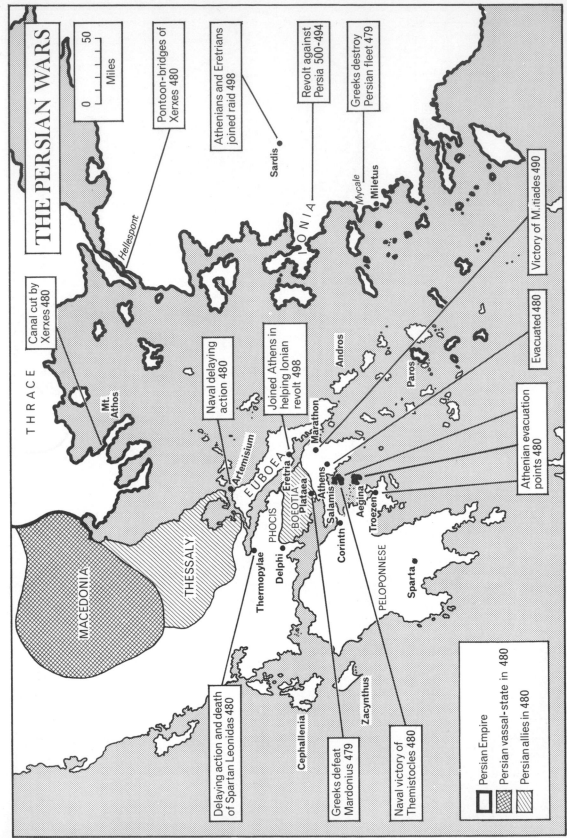

THE PERSIAN WARS

50
Miles
0

Pontoon-bridges of Xerxes 480

Athenians and Eretrians joined raid 498

Revolt against Persia 500-494

Greeks destroy Persian fleet 479

Sardis

Mycale

Miletus

I O N I A

Hellespont

Canal cut by Xerxes 480

Victory of M.:tiades 490

Evacuated 480

T H R A C E

Mt. Athos

Naval delaying action 480

Joined Athens in helping Ionian revolt 498

Andros

Paros

Athenian evacuation points 480

MACEDONIA

Artemisium

EUBOEA

Marathon

Eretria

Athens

Salamis

Aegina

Troezen

THESSALY

PHOCIS

Thermopylae

Delphi

BOEOTIA

Plataea

Corinth

PELOPONNESE

Sparta

Cephallenia

Zacynthus

Delaying action and death of Spartan Leonidas 480

Greeks defeat Mardonius 479

Naval victory of Themistocles 480

Persian Empire

Persian vassal-state in 480

Persian allies in 480

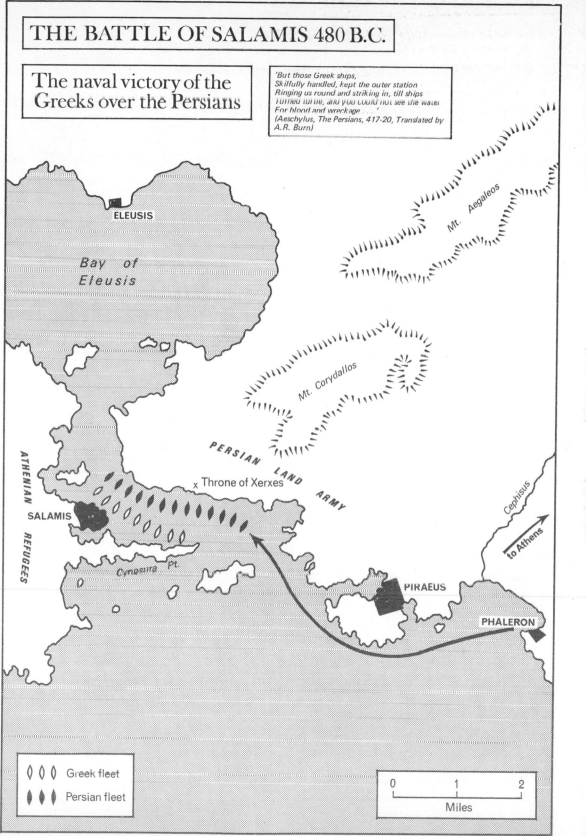

THE BATTLE OF SALAMIS 480 B.C.

The naval victory of the Greeks over the Persians

'But those Greek ships,
Skilfully handled, kept the outer station
Ringing us round and striking in, till ships
Turned turtle, and you could not see the water
For blood and wreckage . . .'
(Aeschylus, The Persians, 417-20, Translated by
A.R. Burn)

ELEUSIS

Bay of Eleusis

Mt. Aegaleos

Mt. Corydallos

PERSIAN LAND ARMY

x Throne of Xerxes

ATHENIAN REFUGEES

SALAMIS

Cynosura Pt.

Cephisus

to Athens

PIRAEUS

PHALERON

◊ ◊ ◊ Greek fleet

◆ ◆ ◆ Persian fleet

0		1		2
Miles

23

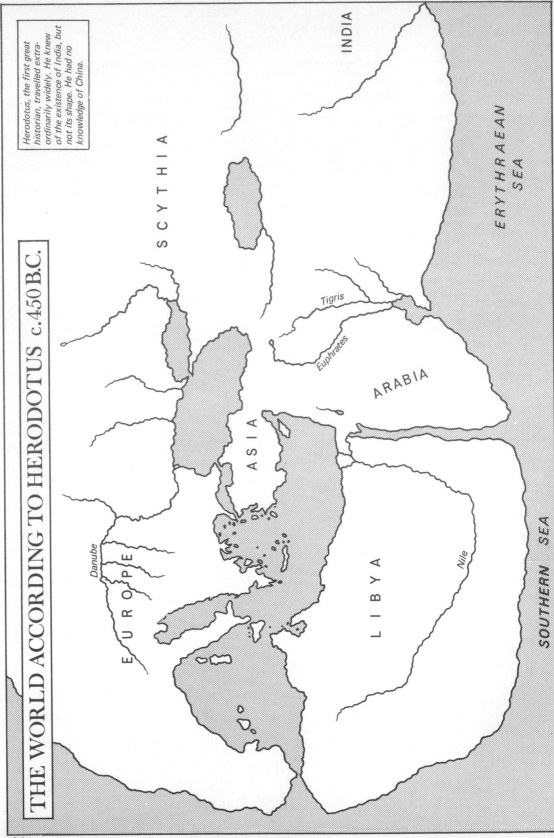

THE WORLD ACCORDING TO HERODOTUS c.450 B.C.

Herodotus, the first great historian, travelled extraordinarily widely. He knew of the existence of India, but not its shape. He had no knowledge of China.

SCYTHIA

INDIA

ERYTHRAEAN SEA

Tigris

Euphrates

ARABIA

ASIA

EUROPE

Danube

LIBYA

Nile

SOUTHERN SEA

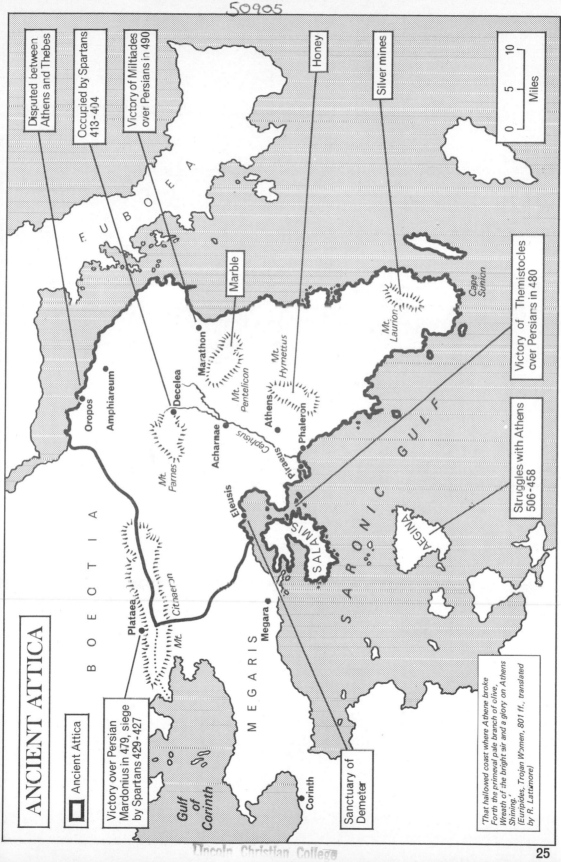

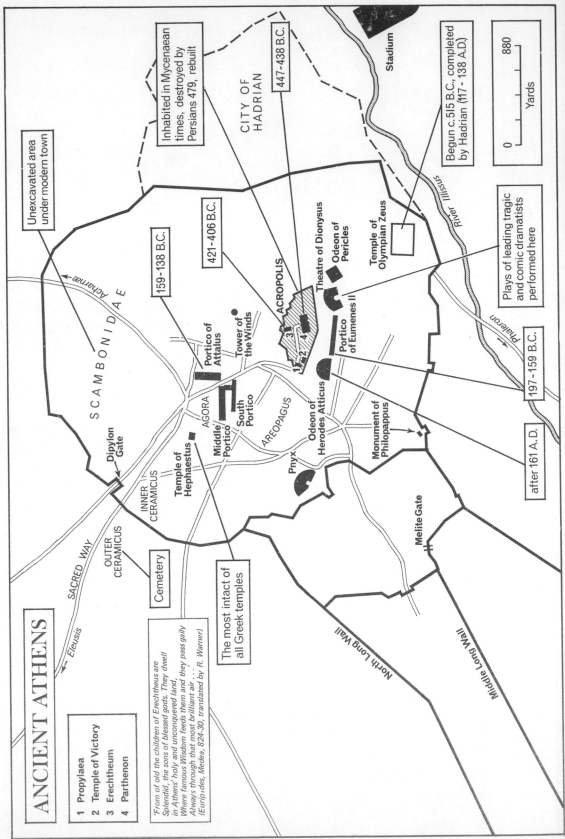

ANCIENT ATHENS

1 Propylaea
2 Temple of Victory
3 Erechtheum
4 Parthenon

'From of old the children of Erechtheus are
Splendid, the sons of blessed gods. They dwell
in Athens' holy and unconquered land,
Where famous Wisdom feeds them and they pass gaily
Always through that most brilliant air . . .'
(Euripides, Medea, 824-30, translated by R. Warner)

The most intact of all Greek temples

Cemetery

Unexcavated area under modern town

Inhabited in Mycenaean times, destroyed by Persians 479, rebuilt

447-438 B.C.

Begun c.515 B.C., completed by Hadrian (117-138 A.D.)

CITY OF HADRIAN

159-138 B.C.

421-406 B.C.

Plays of leading tragic and comic dramatists performed here

197-159 B.C.

after 161 A.D.

Stadium

880

0

Yards

ACROPOLIS

Theatre of Dionysus

Odeon of Pericles

Temple of Olympian Zeus

Portico of Eumenes II

River Illisus

Phaleron

Portico of Attalus

Tower of the Winds

S C A M B O N I D A E

Acharnae

Dipylon Gate

AGORA

Middle Portico

South Portico

Temple of Hephaestus

AREOPAGUS

Pnyx

Odeon of Herodes Atticus

Monument of Philopappus

INNER CERAMICUS

OUTER CERAMICUS

SACRED WAY

Eleusis

Melite Gate

North Long Wall

Middle Long Wall

26

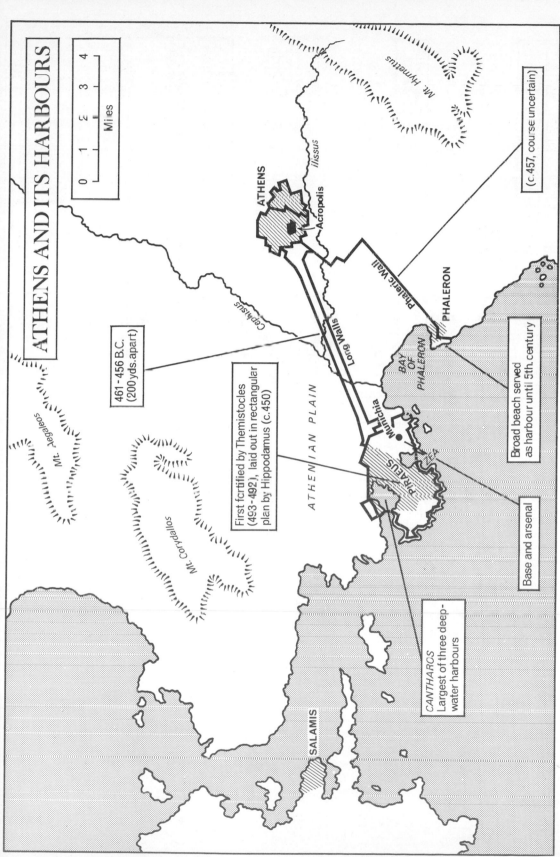

ATHENS AND ITS HARBOURS

Miles
0 1 2 3 4

ATHENS

Acropolis

Ilissus

Mt. Hymettus

(c.457, course uncertain)

Phaleric Wall

PHALERON

461 - 456 B.C.
(200 yds.apart)

Long Walls

Cephisus

Mt. Aegaleos

ATHENIAN PLAIN

Munichia

BAY OF PHALERON

Broad beach served as harbour until 5th century

First fortified by Themistocles (493-492), laid out in rectangular plan by Hippodamus (c.450)

PIRAEUS

Base and arsenal

Mt. Corydallos

CANTHAROS
Largest of three deep-water harbours

SALAMIS

27

THE IMPERIALISM OF FIFTH CENTURY ATHENS

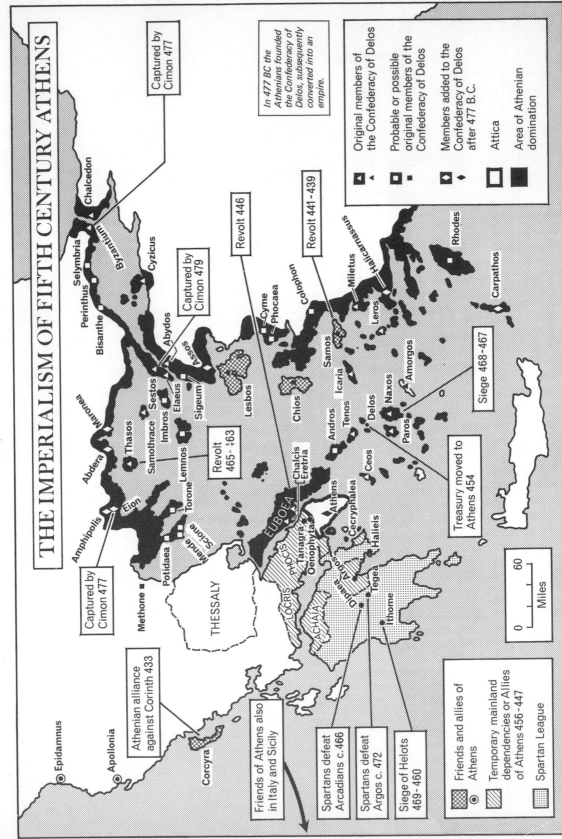

In 477 BC the Athenians founded the Confederacy of Delos, subsequently converted into an empire.

Original members of the Confederacy of Delos

Probable or possible original members of the Confederacy of Delos

Members added to the Confederacy of Delos after 477 B.C.

Attica

Area of Athenian domination

Captured by Cimon 477

Captured by Cimon 479

Captured by Cimon 477

Captured by Cimon 477

Revolt 446

Revolt 441 - 439

Revolt 465 - 463

Siege 468 - 467

Treasury moved to Athens 454

Athenian alliance against Corinth 433

Friends of Athens also as in Italy and Sicily

Spartans defeat Arcadians c. 466

Spartans defeat Argos c. 472

Siege of Helots 469 - 460

Friends and allies of Athens

Temporary mainland dependencies or Allies of Athens 456 - 447

Spartan League

Chalcedon
Selymbria
Perinthus
Bisanthe
Byzantium
Cyzicus
Abydos
Assos
Sestos
Elaeus
Sigeum
Imbros
Samothrace
Thasos
Lemnos
Torone
Maronea
Abdera
Amphipolis
Eion
Methone
Potidaea
Mende
Scione

THESSALY

Cyme
Phocaea
Colophon
Miletus
Halicarnassus
Rhodes
Carpathos
Samos
Icaria
Leros
Amorgos
Naxos
Paros
Delos
Tenos
Andros
Ceos
Chios
Lesbos

EUBOEA
Chalcis
Eretria
Athens
Cecryphalea
Halieis
LOCRIS
PHOCIS
Tanagra
Oenophyta
Aegina
Megara
ACHAIA
Tegea
Ithome

Corcyra

Epidamnus
Apollonia

0   60
Miles

28

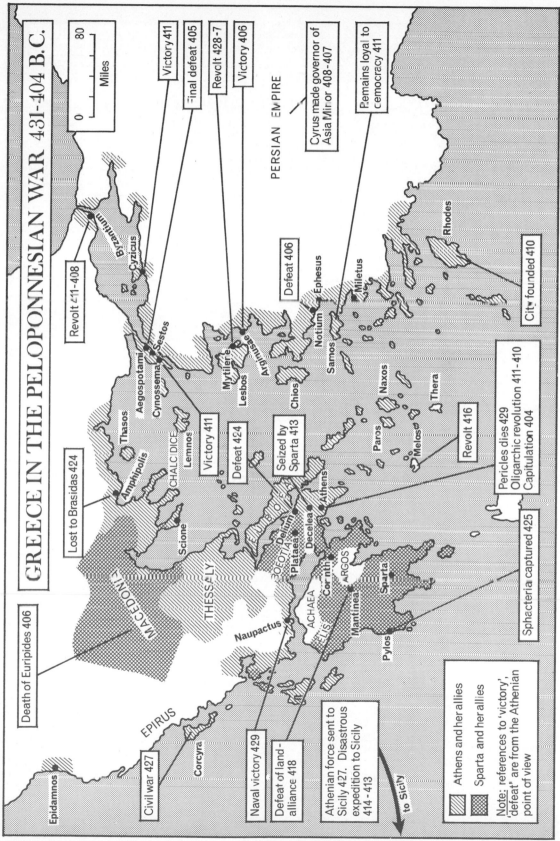

GREECE IN THE PELOPONNESIAN WAR 431–404 B.C.

0 ___ 80 Miles

PERSIAN EMPIRE

Cyrus made governor of Asia Minor 408–407

Remains loyal to democracy 411

Victory 411

Final defeat 405

Revolt 428–7

Victory 406

Revolt 411–408

Defeat 406

City founded 410

Rhodes

Byzantium

Cyzicus

Aegospotami

Sestos

Cynossema

Ephesus

Notium

Miletus

Samos

Mytilene

Lesbos

Arginusae

Chios

Thasos

Lemnos

CHALCIDICE

Amphipolis

Scione

Naxos

Paros

Thera

Melos

Victory 411

Defeat 424

Seized by Sparta 413

Revolt 416

Lost to Brasidas 424

Pericles dies 429
Oligarchic revolution 411–410
Capitulation 404

MACEDONIA

THESSALY

EPIRUS

Corcyra

Civil war 427

Epidamnos

Death of Euripides 406

Naupactus

BOEOTIA

EUBOEA

Delium

Plataea

Decelea

Athens

Corinth

ARGOS

ACHAEA

ELIS

Mantinea

Sparta

Pylos

Sphacteria captured 425

Naval victory 429

Defeat of land-alliance 418

Athenian force sent to Sicily 427. Disastrous expedition to Sicily 414–413

to Sicily

Athens and her allies

Sparta and her allies

Note: references to 'victory', 'defeat' are from the Athenian point of view

29

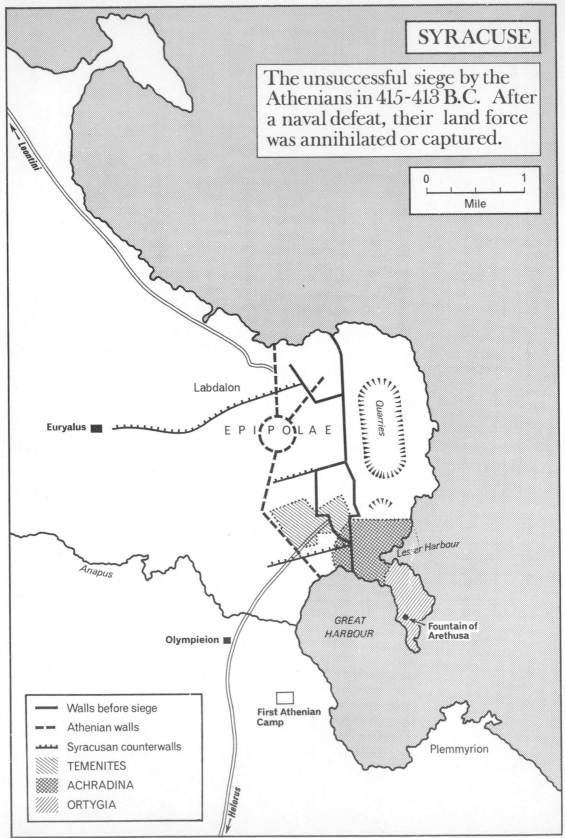

SYRACUSE

The unsuccessful siege by the Athenians in 415-413 B.C. After a naval defeat, their land force was annihilated or captured.

0 ——————— 1
Mile

Leontini

Labdalon

Euryalus

E P I P O L A E

Quarries

Anapus

Lesser Harbour

GREAT
HARBOUR

Fountain of
Arethusa

Olympieion

First Athenian
Camp

Plemmyrion

Helorus

Walls before siege
Athenian walls
Syracusan counterwalls
TEMENITES
ACHRADINA
ORTYGIA

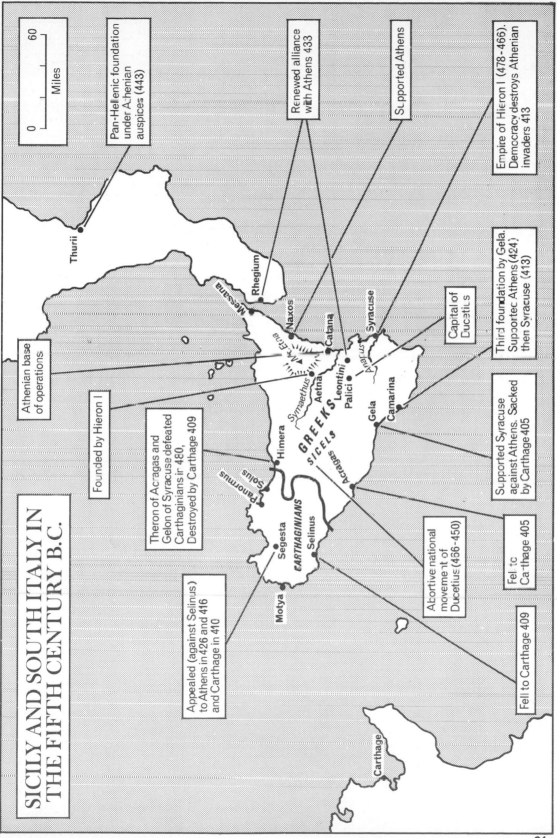

SICILY AND SOUTH ITALY IN THE FIFTH CENTURY B.C.

0   60
Miles

Pan-Hellenic foundation under Athenian auspices (443)

Renewed alliance with Athens 433

Supported Athens

Empire of Hieron I (478-466). Democracy destroys Athenian invaders 413

Athenian base of operations

Founded by Hieron I

Theron of Acragas and Gelon of Syracuse defeated Carthaginians in 480. Destroyed by Carthage 409

Capital of Ducetius

Third foundation by Gela. Supported Athens (424) then Syracuse (413)

Supported Syracuse against Athens. Sacked by Carthage 405

Appealed (against Selinus) to Athens in 426 and 416 and Carthage in 410

Abortive national movement of Ducetius (466-450)

Fell to Carthage 405

Fell to Carthage 409

Thurii

Messana

Rhegium

Naxos

Catana

Syracuse

Symaethus R.

Aetna

Mt Etna

Leontini

Palici

Anapus R.

Gela

Camarina

Acragas

Himera

Panormus

Solus

GREEKS

SICELS

Segesta

Selinus

CARTHAGINIANS

Motya

Carthage

31

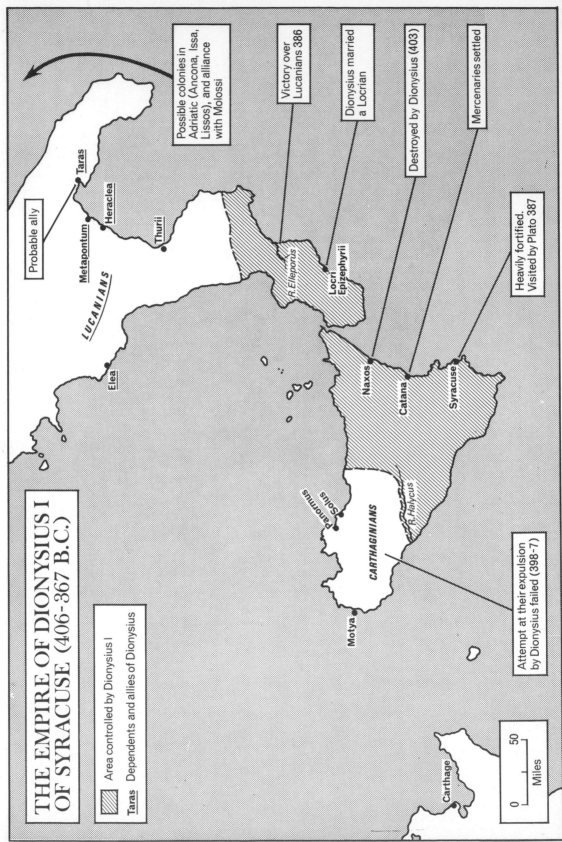

THE EMPIRE OF DIONYSIUS I OF SYRACUSE (406-367 B.C.)

Area controlled by Dionysius I

Taras Dependents and allies of Dionysius

Probable ally

Possible colonies in Adriatic (Ancona, Issa, Lissos), and alliance with Molossi

Victory over Lucanians 386

Dionysius married a Locrian

Destroyed by Dionysius (403)

Mercenaries settled

Heavily fortified. Visited by Plato 387

Attempt at their expulsion by Dionysius failed (398-7)

Taras

Heraclea

Metapontum

Thurii

LUCANIANS

R. Elleporus

Locri Epizephyrii

Elea

Naxos

Catana

Syracuse

Panormus

Solus

CARTHAGINIANS

R. Halycus

Motya

Carthage

Miles

0   50

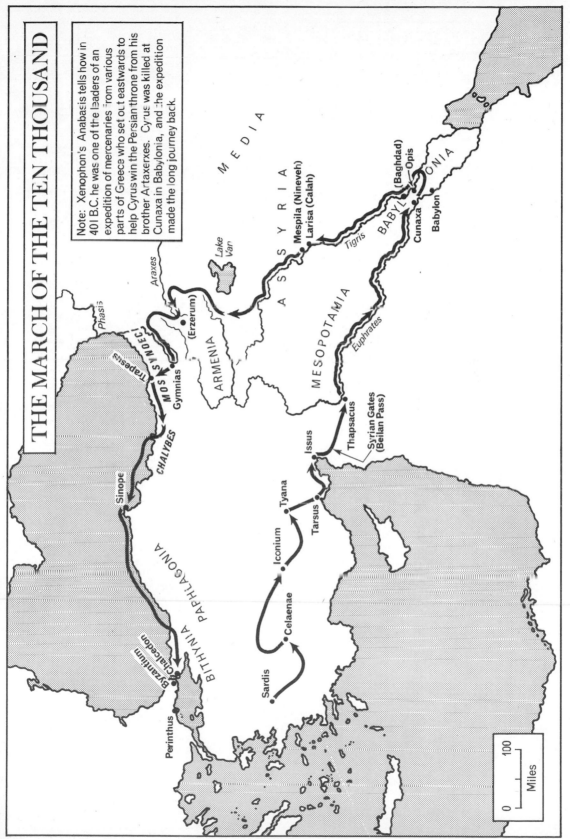

THE MARCH OF THE TEN THOUSAND

Note: Xenophon's *Anabasis* tells how in 401 B.C. he was one of the leaders of an expedition of mercenaries from various parts of Greece who set out eastwards to help Cyrus win the Persian throne from his brother Artaxerxes. Cyrus was killed at Cunaxa in Babylonia, and the expedition made the long journey back.

MEDIA

ASSYRIA

Mespila (Nineveh)
Larisa (Calah)

Tigris

BABYL   ONIA

(Baghdad)
Opis

Cunaxa

Babylon

Araxes

Lake Van

Phasis

(Erzerum)

ARMENIA

MESOPOTAMIA

Euphrates

MOSSYNOECI

Trapesus

Gymnias

CHALYBES

Thapsacus

Issus

Syrian Gates
(Beilan Pass)

Sinope

Tyana

Iconium

Tarsus

BITHYNIA PAPHLAGONIA

Celaenae

Byzantium
Chalcedon

Perinthus

Sardis

100

0

Miles

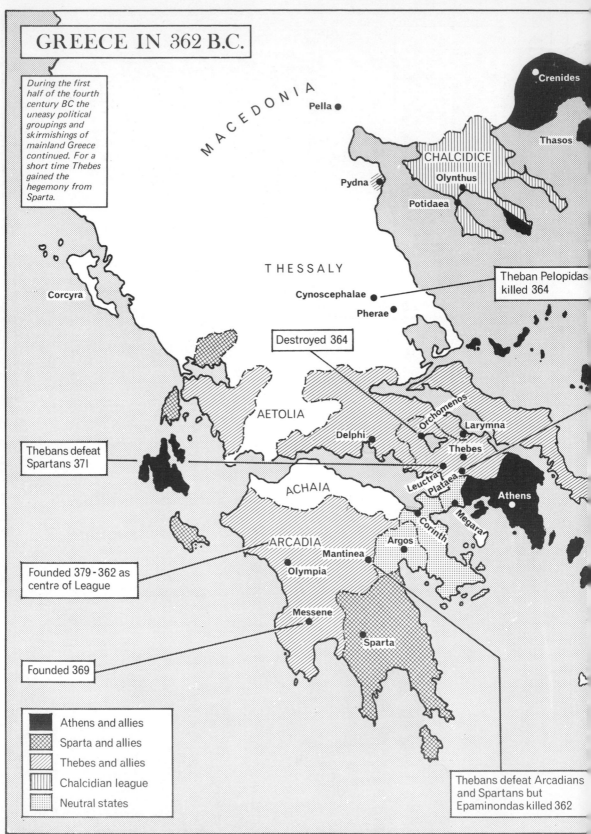

GREECE IN 362 B.C.

During the first half of the fourth century BC the uneasy political groupings and skirmishings of mainland Greece continued. For a short time Thebes gained the hegemony from Sparta.

MACEDONIA

Crenides

Pella

Thasos

CHALCIDICE

Pydna

Olynthus

Potidaea

THESSALY

Theban Pelopidas killed 364

Cynoscephalae

Pherae

Destroyed 364

Corcyra

AETOLIA

Delphi

Orchomenos

Larymna

Thebes

Thebans defeat Spartans 371

Leuctra

Plataea

Athens

ACHAIA

Corinth

Megara

Argos

ARCADIA

Mantinea

Founded 379-362 as centre of League

Olympia

Messene

Sparta

Founded 369

Thebans defeat Arcadians and Spartans but Epaminondas killed 362

■	Athens and allies
▨	Sparta and allies
▧	Thebes and allies
▥	Chalcidian league
▦	Neutral states

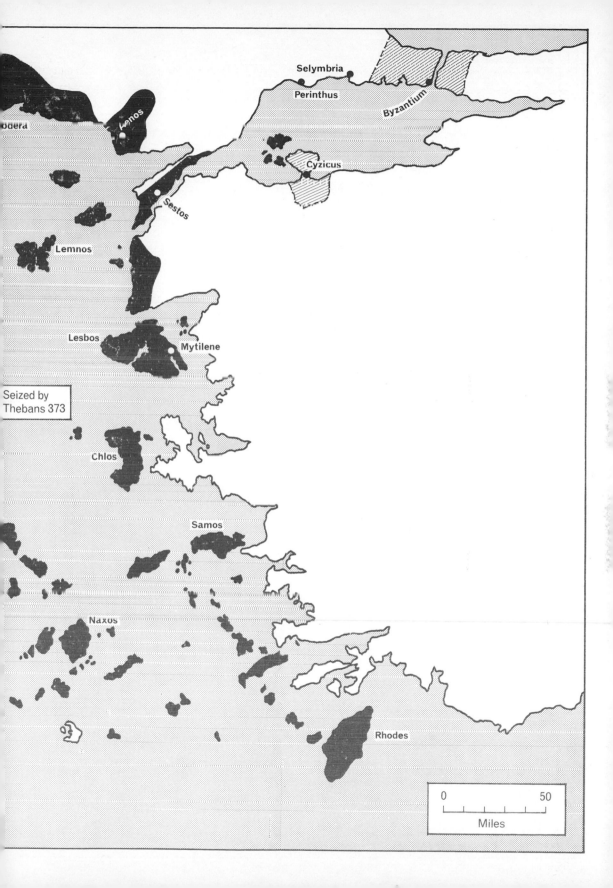

Selymbria

Perinthus

Byzantium

Cyzicus

odera

Lemnos

Sestos

Lemnos

Lesbos

Mytilene

Seized by
Thebans 373

Chios

Samos

Naxos

Rhodes

0   50

Miles

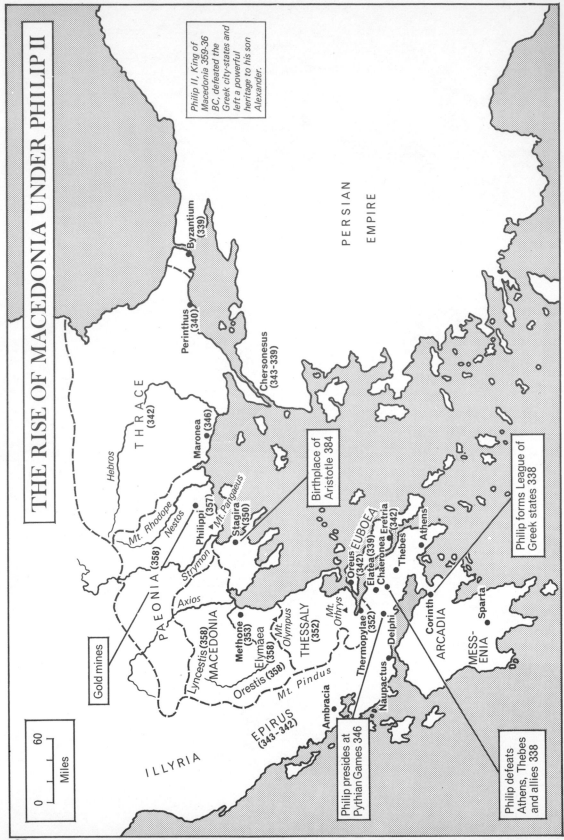

THE RISE OF MACEDONIA UNDER PHILIP II

Philip II, King of Macedonia 359-36 BC, defeated the Greek city-states and left a powerful heritage to his son Alexander.

PERSIAN EMPIRE

Byzantium (339)

Perinthus (340)

Chersonesus (343-339)

THRACE (342)

Hebros

Mt. Rhodope

Maronea (346)

Nestos

Philippi (357)

Mt. Pangaeus (350)

Stagira

Birthplace of Aristotle 384

EUBOEA

Oreus (342)

Elatea (339)

Eretria (342)

Chaeronea

Thebes

Athens

Philip forms League of Greek states 338

Strymon

PAEONIA (358)

Axios

Mt. Olympus

THESSALY (352)

Mt. Othrys

Thermopylae (352)

Delphi

Corinth

Sparta

ARCADIA

MESS-ENIA

Gold mines

Lyncestis (358)

Methone (353)

Elymaea

MACEDONIA

Orestis (358)

Mt. Pindus

Naupactus

Philip defeats Athens, Thebes and allies 338

EPIRUS (343-342)

Ambracia

Philip presides at Pythian Games 346

ILLYRIA

0   60
Miles

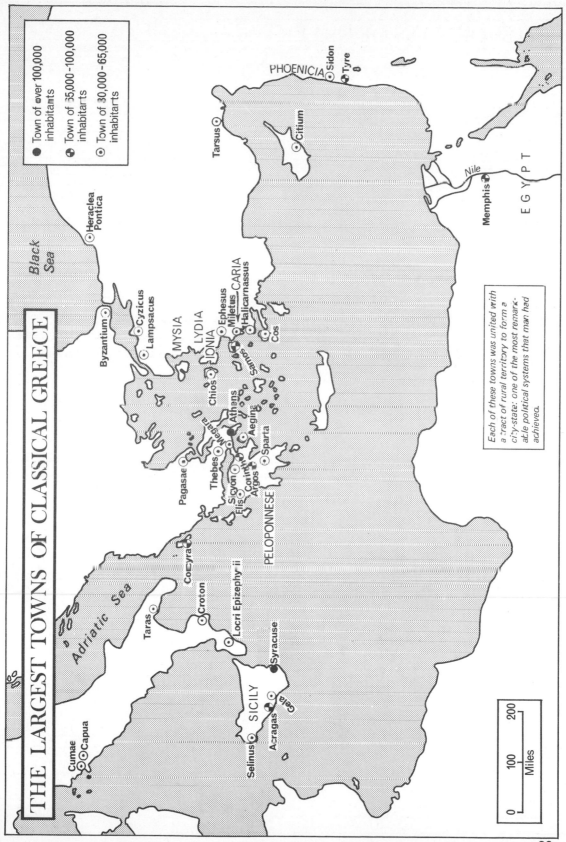

THE LARGEST TOWNS OF CLASSICAL GREECE

Town of over 100,000 inhabitants

Town of 35,000 – 100,000 inhabitarts

Town of 30,000 – 65,000 inhabitarts

Each of these towns was united with a tract of rural territory to form a city-state: one of the most remarkable political systems that man had achieved.

PHOENICIA
Sidon
Tyre

Tarsus

Citium

Nile

EGYPT

Memphis

Black Sea

Heraclea Pontica

Cyzicus
Lampsacus

Byzantium

MYSIA
LYDIA
IONIA
CARIA
Ephesus
Miletus
Halicarnassus
Cos
Samos

Chios

Athens
Aegina
Sparta

Pagasae

Thebes
Sicyon
Elis
Corinth
Argos

PELOPONNESE

Corcyra

Croton

Locri Epizephyrii

Taras

Syracuse

SICILY
Gela
Acragas
Selinus

Adriatic Sea

Cumae
Capua

0   100   200
Miles

36

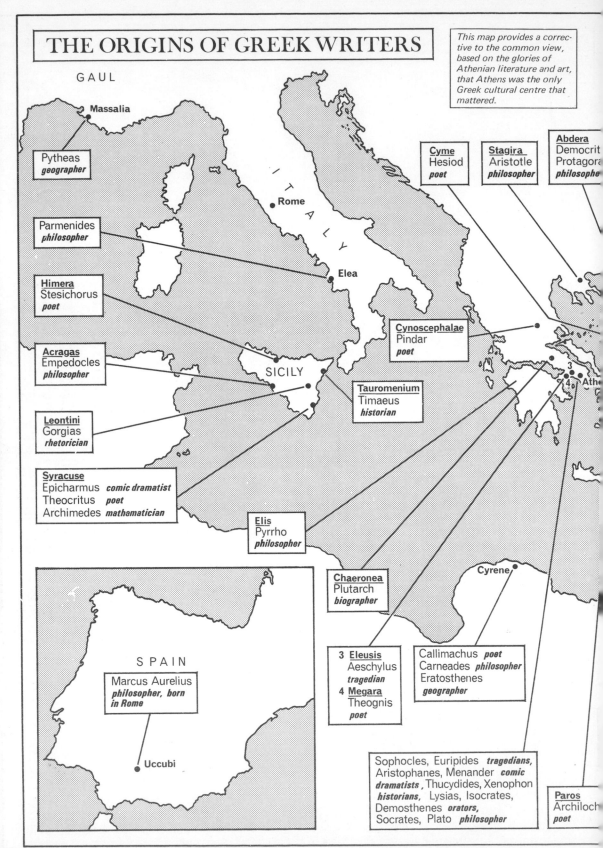

THE ORIGINS OF GREEK WRITERS

This map provides a corrective to the common view, based on the glories of Athenian literature and art, that Athens was the only Greek cultural centre that mattered.

GAUL

Massalia

Pytheas
geographer

ITALY

Rome

Parmenides
philosopher

Elea

Himera
Stesichorus
poet

Acragas
Empedocles
philosopher

SICILY

Leontini
Gorgias
rhetorician

Syracuse
Epicharmus *comic dramatist*
Theocritus *poet*
Archimedes *mathematician*

Cyme
Hesiod
poet

Stagira
Aristotle
philosopher

Abdera
Democrit
Protagora
philosophe

Cynoscephalae
Pindar
poet

Tauromenium
Timaeus
historian

3
4 Ath

Elis
Pyrrho
philosopher

Chaeronea
Plutarch
biographer

Cyrene

SPAIN

Marcus Aurelius
philosopher, born in Rome

Uccubi

3 **Eleusis**
Aeschylus
tragedian
4 **Megara**
Theognis
poet

Callimachus *poet*
Carneades *philosopher*
Eratosthenes
geographer

Sophocles, Euripides *tragedians*,
Aristophanes, Menander *comic dramatists*, Thucydides, Xenophon
historians, Lysias, Isocrates,
Demosthenes *orators*,
Socrates, Plato *philosopher*

Paros
Archiloch
poet

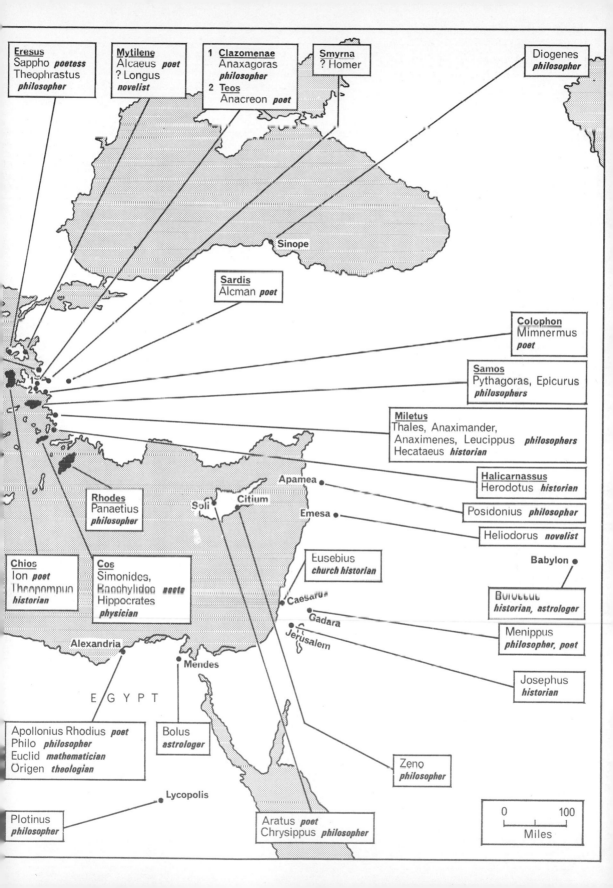

Eresus
Sappho *poetess*
Theophrastus
philosopher

Mytilene
Alcaeus *poet*
? Longus
novelist

1 **Clazomenae**
Anaxagoras
philosopher
2 **Teos**
Anacreon *poet*

Smyrna
? Homer

Diogenes
philosopher

Sinope

Sardis
Alcman *poet*

Colophon
Mimnermus
poet

Samos
Pythagoras, Epicurus
philosophers

Miletus
Thales, Anaximander,
Anaximenes, Leucippus *philosophers*
Hecataeus *historian*

Apamea

Citium

Soli

Halicarnassus
Herodotus *historian*

Posidonius *philosopher*

Emesa

Heliodorus *novelist*

Rhodes
Panaetius
philosopher

Chios
Ion *poet*
Theopompus
historian

Cos
Simonides,
Bacchylides *poets*
Hippocrates
physician

Eusebius
church historian

Babylon

Berossus
historian, astrologer

Caesarea

Gadara

Menippus
philosopher, poet

Jerusalem

Josephus
historian

Alexandria

Mendes

E G Y P T

Apollonius Rhodius *poet*
Philo *philosopher*
Euclid *mathematician*
Origen *theologian*

Bolus
astrologer

Zeno
philosopher

Lycopolis

Plotinus
philosopher

Aratus *poet*
Chrysippus *philosopher*

0   100

Miles

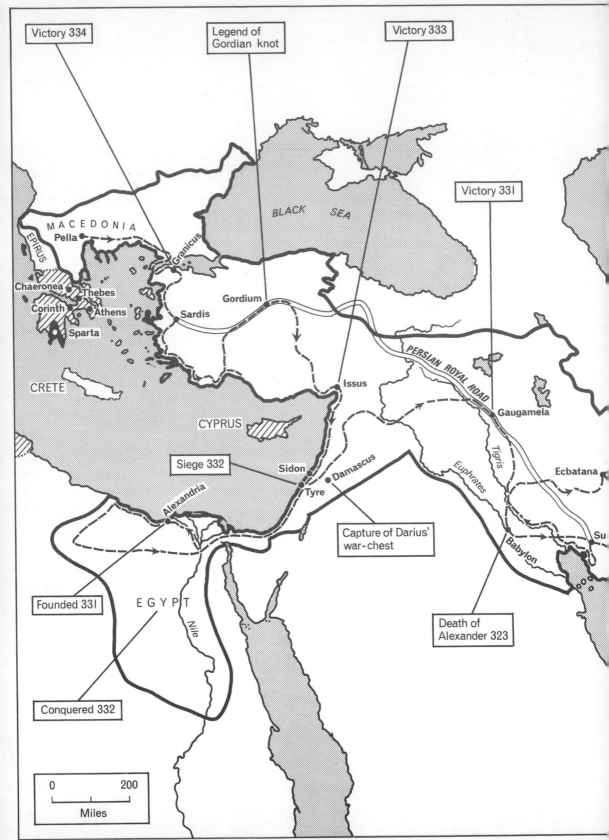

Victory 334

Legend of Gordian knot

Victory 333

Victory 331

MACEDONIA

EPIRUS

Pella

Chaeronea

Thebes

Corinth

Athens

Sparta

CRETE

BLACK SEA

Granicus

Gordium

Sardis

CYPRUS

Issus

PERSIAN ROYAL ROAD

Gaugamela

Ecbatana

Siege 332

Sidon

Damascus

Tyre

Capture of Darius' war-chest

Euphrates

Tigris

Babylon

Su

Alexandria

Founded 331

Conquered 332

EGYPT

Nile

Death of Alexander 323

0   200
Miles

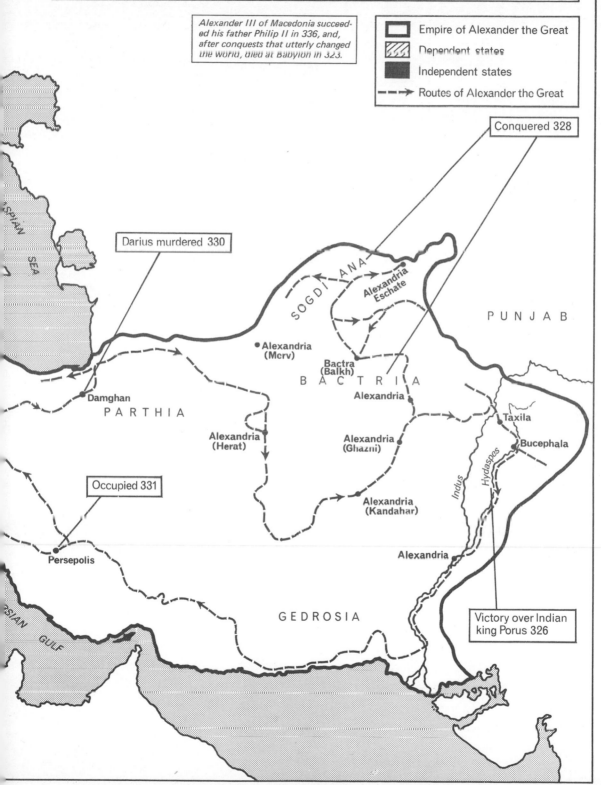

THE CONQUESTS OF ALEXANDER THE GREAT

Alexander III of Macedonia succeeded his father Philip II in 336, and, after conquests that utterly changed the world, died at Babylon in 323.

Empire of Alexander the Great
Dependent states
Independent states
→ Routes of Alexander the Great

Conquered 328

Darius murdered 330

CASPIAN SEA

SOGDIANA

Alexandria Eschate

PUNJAB

Alexandria (Merv)

Bactra (Balkh)

BACTRIA

Alexandria

Damghan

PARTHIA

Taxila

Bucephala

Alexandria (Herat)

Alexandria (Ghazni)

Occupied 331

Indus

Hydaspes

Alexandria (Kandahar)

Persepolis

Alexandria

PERSIAN GULF

GEDROSIA

Victory over Indian king Porus 326

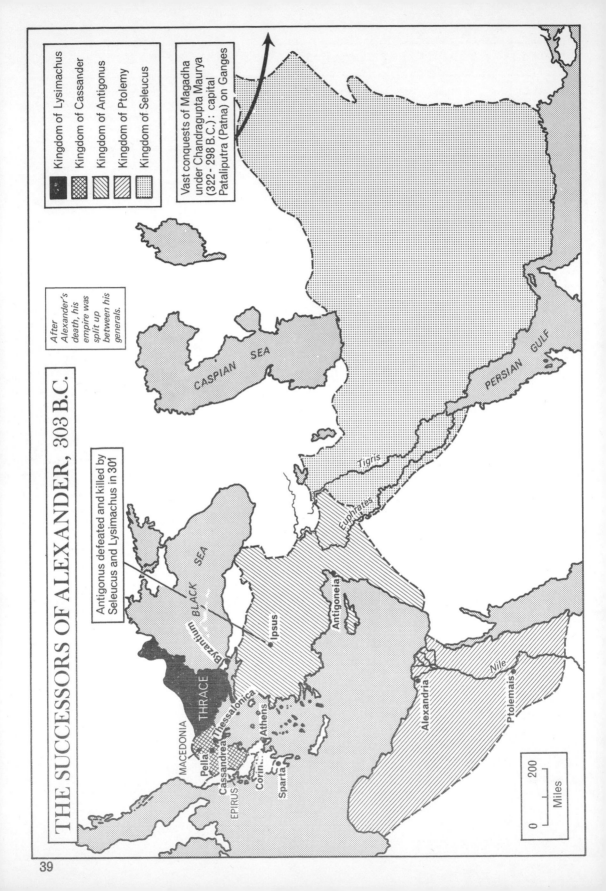

THE SUCCESSORS OF ALEXANDER, 303 B.C.

Kingdom of Lysimachus
Kingdom of Cassander
Kingdom of Antigonus
Kingdom of Ptolemy
Kingdom of Seleucus

Vast conquests of Magadha under Chandragupta Maurya (322 - 298 B.C.): capital Pataliputra (Patna) on Ganges

After Alexander's death, his empire was split up between his generals.

Antigonus defeated and killed by Seleucus and Lysimachus in 301

CASPIAN SEA

PERSIAN GULF

Tigris

Euphrates

BLACK SEA

Byzantium

Ipsus

Antigoneia

Nile

THRACE

MACEDONIA

Thessalonica

Pella

Cassandrea

Athens

Corinth

Sparta

EPIRUS

Alexandria

Ptolemais

0   200

Miles

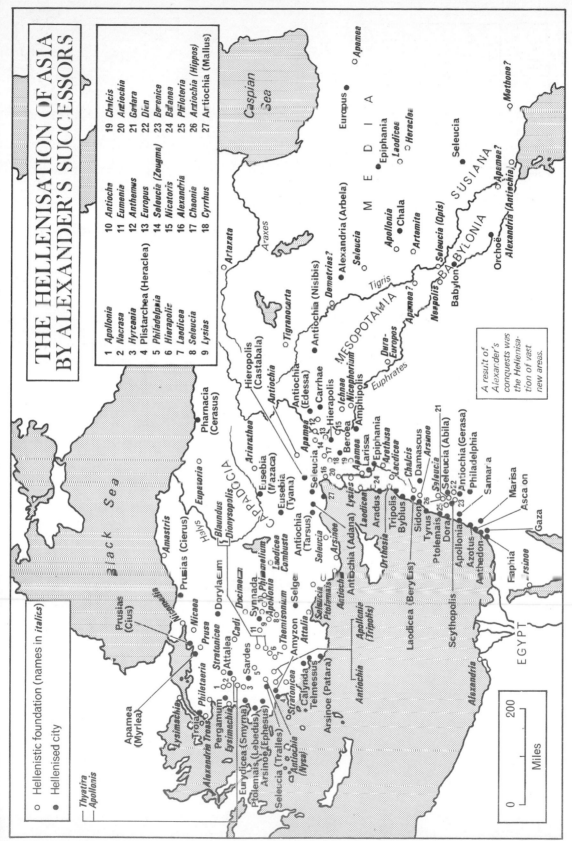

THE HELLENISATION OF ASIA BY ALEXANDER'S SUCCESSORS

1	*Apollonia*	10	*Antiocha*	19	*Chlcis*
2	*Nacrasa*	11	*Eumenia*	20	*Antiochia*
3	*Hyrcania*	12	*Anthemus*	21	*Gerara*
4	Plistarchea (Heraclea)	13	*Europus*	22	*Dien*
5	*Philadelphia*	14	*Seleucia (Zeugma)*	23	*Berenice*
6	*Hierapolis*	15	*Nicatoris*	24	*Baanea*
7	*Laodicea*	16	*Alexandria*	25	*Philoteria*
8	*Seleucia*	17	*Chaonia*	26	Artiochia (Hippos)
9	*Lysias*	18	*Cyrrhus*	27	Artiochia (Mallus)

○ Hellenistic foundation (names in *italics*)

● Hellenised city

Thyatira
Apollonis

A result of Alexander's conquests was the Hellenisation of vast new areas.

Miles

0   200

40

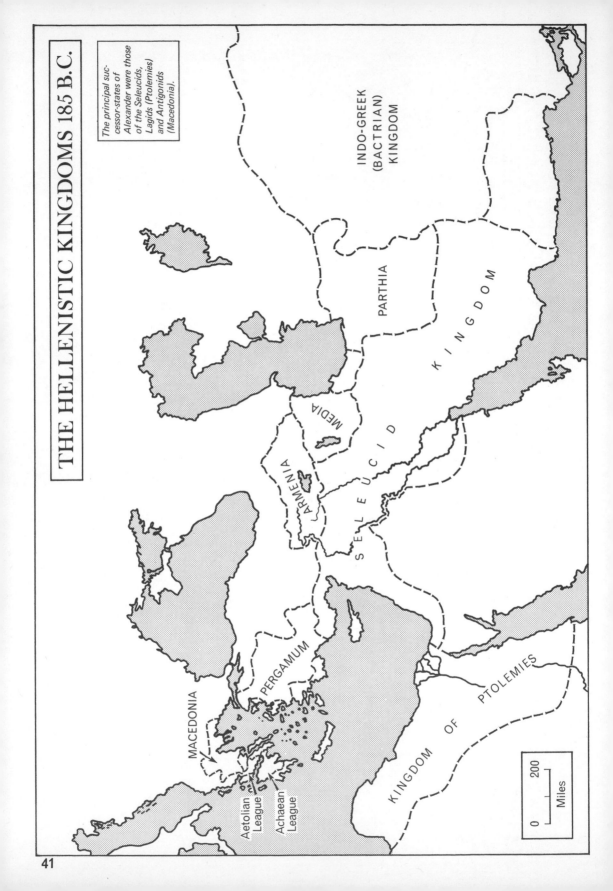

THE HELLENISTIC KINGDOMS 185 B.C.

The principal successor-states of Alexander were those of the Seleucids, Lagids (Ptolemies) and Antigonids (Macedonia).

INDO-GREEK (BACTRIAN) KINGDOM

PARTHIA

MEDIA

ARMENIA

SELEUCID KINGDOM

PERGAMUM

MACEDONIA

Aetolian League

Achaean League

KINGDOM OF PTOLEMIES

200

0

Miles

41

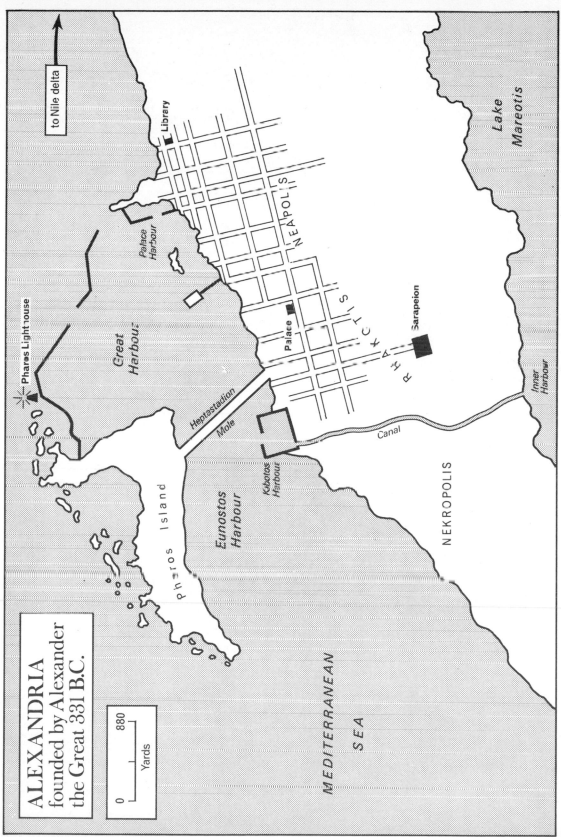

ALEXANDRIA
founded by Alexander
the Great 331 B.C.

0   880
Yards

to Nile delta

Library

Palace Harbour

Pharos Lighthouse

Great Harbour

Heptastadion
Mole

NEAPOLIS

Palace

R H A K O T I S

Sarapeion

Lake Mareotis

Inner Harbour

Canal

Pharos Island

Eunostos Harbour

Kibotos Harbour

NEKROPOLIS

MEDITERRANEAN SEA

42

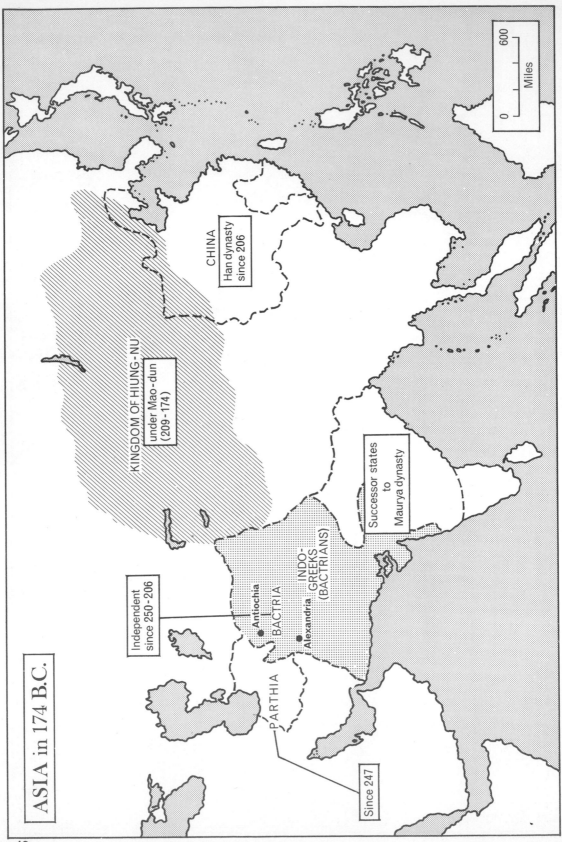

ASIA in 174 B.C.

KINGDOM OF HIUNG - NU
under Mao - dun
(209 - 174)

CHINA
Han dynasty
since 206

Successor states
to
Maurya dynasty

Independent
since 250 - 206

INDO-
GREEKS
(BACTRIANS)

BACTRIA

Antiochia

Alexandria

PARTHIA

Since 247

600

Miles

0

43

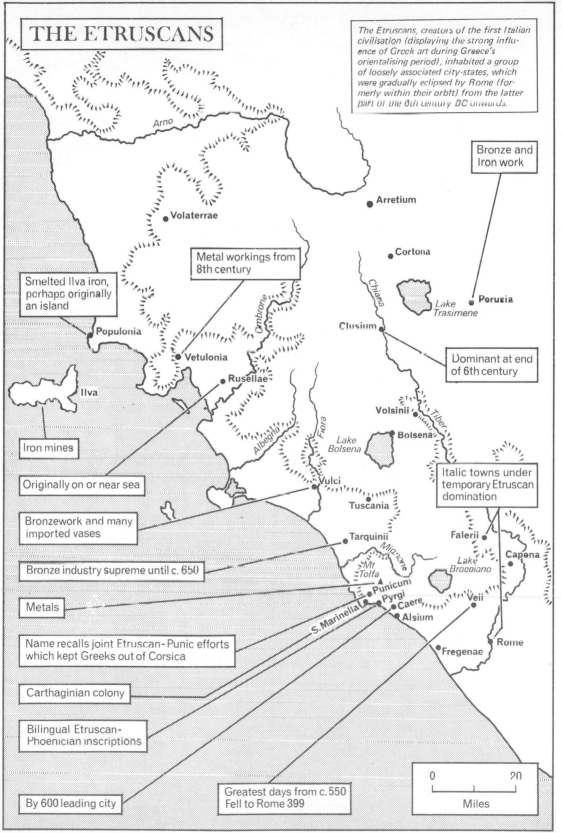

THE ETRUSCANS

The Etruscans, creators of the first Italian civilisation (displaying the strong influence of Greek art during Greece's orientalising period), inhabited a group of loosely associated city-states, which were gradually eclipsed by Rome (formerly within their orbit) from the latter part of the 8th century BC onwards.

Arno

Bronze and Iron work

• **Arretium**

• **Volaterrae**

• **Cortona**

Metal workings from 8th century

Chiana

Lake Trasimene

• **Perusia**

Smelted Ilva iron, perhaps originally an island

Ombrone

Clusium

• **Populonia**

Dominant at end of 6th century

• **Vetulonia**

• **Rusellae**

Fiora

Ilva

Albegna

Volsinii

Tiber

Bolsena

Lake Bolsena

Iron mines

Originally on or near sea

Italic towns under temporary Etruscan domination

Vulci

Bronzework and many imported vases

Tuscania

• **Falerii**

Bronze industry supreme until c. 650

• **Tarquinii**

Marta

Lake Bracciano

• **Capena**

Mt Tolfa

Metals

Punicum

Pyrgi

• **Veii**

Name recalls joint Etruscan-Punic efforts which kept Greeks out of Corsica

S.Marinella

• **Caere**

• **Alsium**

Carthaginian colony

• **Rome**

• **Fregenae**

Bilingual Etruscan-Phoenician inscriptions

0   20

By 600 leading city

Greatest days from c. 550 Fell to Rome 399

Miles

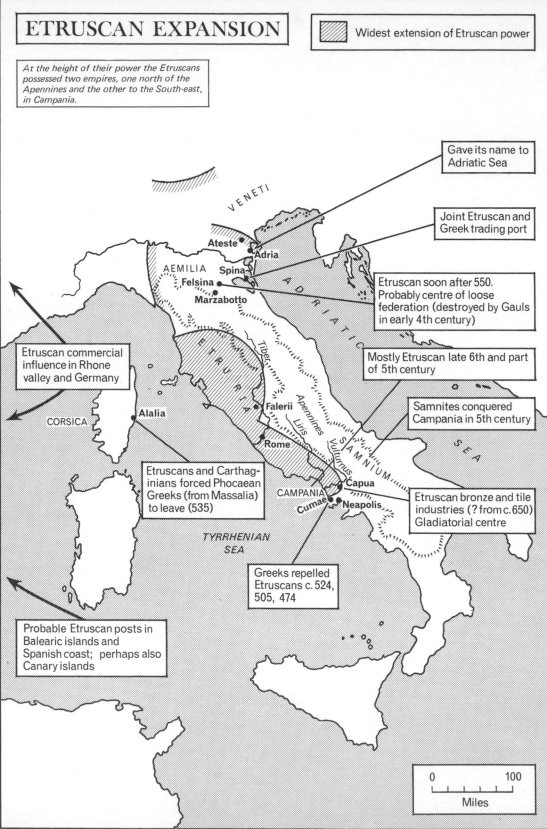

ETRUSCAN EXPANSION

Widest extension of Etruscan power

At the height of their power the Etruscans possessed two empires, one north of the Apennines and the other to the South-east, in Campania.

VENETI

Gave its name to Adriatic Sea

Joint Etruscan and Greek trading port

Ateste

Adria

AEMILIA

Spina

Felsina

Marzabotto

ADRIATIC

Etruscan soon after 550. Probably centre of loose federation (destroyed by Gauls in early 4th century)

ETRURIA

Tiber

Apennines

Liris

Mostly Etruscan late 6th and part of 5th century

Etruscan commercial influence in Rhone valley and Germany

CORSICA

Alalia

Falerii

Rome

Samnites conquered Campania in 5th century

SEA

Etruscans and Carthaginians forced Phocaean Greeks (from Massalia) to leave (535)

Volturnus

SAMNIUM

Capua

CAMPANIA

Cumae

Neapolis

Etruscan bronze and tile industries (? from c.650) Gladiatorial centre

TYRRHENIAN SEA

Greeks repelled Etruscans c. 524, 505, 474

Probable Etruscan posts in Balearic islands and Spanish coast; perhaps also Canary islands

0	100

Miles

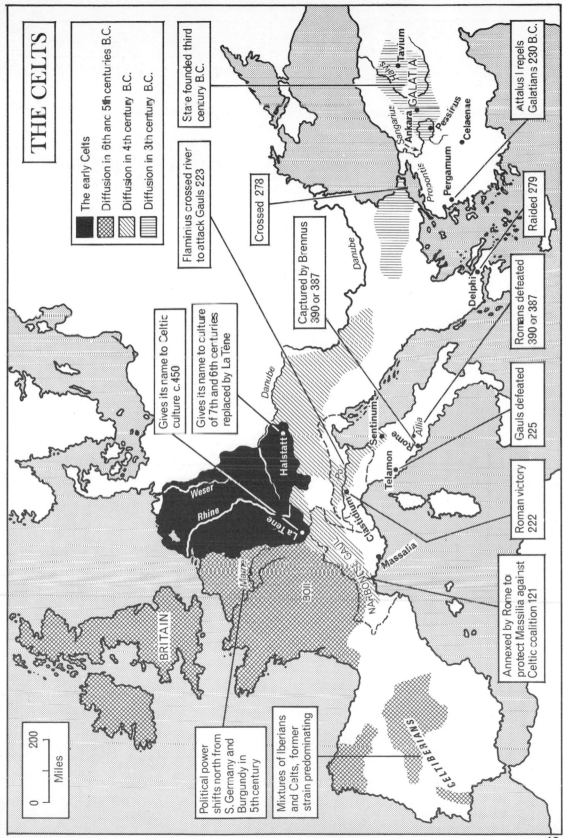

THE CELTS

The early Celts

- ■ The early Celts
- ▨ Diffusion in 6th and 5th centuries B.C.
- ▩ Diffusion in 4th century B.C.
- ▤ Diffusion in 3rd century B.C.

State founded third century B.C.

Flaminius crossed river to attack Gauls 223

Crossed 278

Captured by Brennus 390 or 387

Gives its name to Celtic culture c.450

Gives its name to culture of 7th and 6th centuries replaced by La Tène

Political power shifts north from S. Germany and Burgundy in 5th century

Mixtures of Iberians and Celts, former strain predominating

Attalus I repels Galatians 230 B.C.

Raided 279

Romans defeated 390 or 387

Gauls defeated 225

Roman victory 222

Annexed by Rome to protect Massilia against Celtic coalition 121

Tavium

GALATIA

Ankara

Pessinus

Celaenae

Sangarius

Pergamum

Propontis

Delphi

Danube

Danube

BRITAIN

Halstatt

Weser

Rhine

La Tène

Maine

BOII

GAUL

NARBONENSIS

Sentinum

Rome

Allia

Telamon

Clastidium

Lumpitinum

Massilia

Po

CELTIBERIANS

0   200
Miles

46

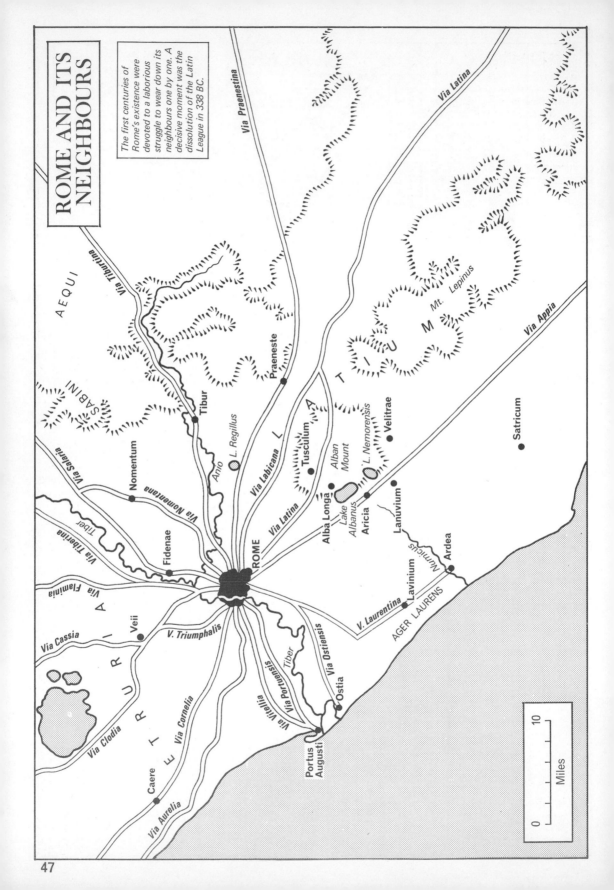

ROME AND ITS NEIGHBOURS

The first centuries of Rome's existence were devoted to a laborious struggle to wear down its neighbours one by one. A decisive moment was the dissolution of the Latin League in 338 BC.

Via Praenestina

Via Latina

AEQUI

Via Tiburtina

SABINI

Via Salaria

Via Nomentana

Via Tiberina

Via Flaminia

Via Cassia

Via Clodia

Via Cornelia

Via Aurelia

E T R U R I A

Caere

Veii

V. Triumphalis

Fidenae

Nomentum

Tibur

Praeneste

Anio

L. Regillus

Via Labicana

Via Latina

Tusculum

Alban Mount

Alba Longa

Lake Albanus

Aricia

L. Nemorensis

Velitrae

Mt. Lepinus

L A T I U M

Satricum

Lanuvium

Numicius

Ardea

Lavinium

V. Laurentina

AGER LAURENS

Via Appia

ROME

Tiber

Via Vitellia

Via Portuensis

Via Ostiensis

Ostia

Portus Augusti

0   10

Miles

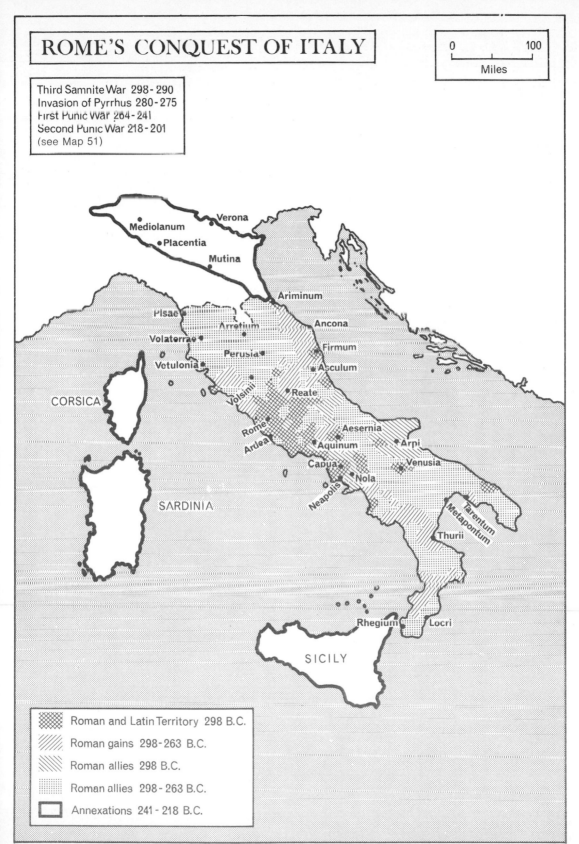

ROME'S CONQUEST OF ITALY

0   100
Miles

Third Samnite War 298-290
Invasion of Pyrrhus 280-275
First Punic War 264-241
Second Punic War 218-201
(see Map 51)

Verona
Mediolanum
Placentia
Mutina

Ariminum

Pisae
Arretium
Ancona
Volaterrae
Perusia
Firmum
Vetulonia
Asculum

CORSICA

Volsinii
Reate

Rome
Aesernia
Ardea
Aquinum
Arpi
Capua
Venusia
Nola
Neapolis

SARDINIA

Tarentum
Metapontum
Thurii

Rhegium
Locri

SICILY

- Roman and Latin Territory 298 B.C.
- Roman gains 298-263 B.C.
- Roman allies 298 B.C.
- Roman allies 298-263 B.C.
- Annexations 241-218 B.C.

THE ROADS OF ROMAN ITALY

0 — 100
Miles

Augusta Praetoria
Segusio
Mediolanum
Placentia
Cremona
Verona
Aquileia
⑥
①
Dertona
Mantua
⑥
Genua
Po
①
Ravenna
⑧
Luna
Florentia
Ariminum
Fanum Fortunae
Pisae
Arretium
Vada Volaterrana
⑪
④
⑬
Truentum
Reate
Aternum
③
Tiber
Tibur
⑦
Corfinium
ROME
Anagnia
CORSICA
②
⑤
Fregellae
Beneventum
Tarracina
Capua
Canusium
⑩
Cales
Casilinum
Venusia
②
Brundisium
Neapolis
Tarentum
⑫
SARDINIA
⑨
TYRRHENIAN SEA
Rhegium
SICILY

ADRIATIC SEA

①	Via Aemilia (187 B.C.)	⑧	Via Julia Augusta
②	Via Appia (312 - 244 B.C.)	⑨	Via Domitiana
③	Via Aurelia	⑩	Via Trajana
④	Via Flaminia (220 B.C.)	⑪	Via Cassia
⑤	Via Latina	⑫	Via Popillia
⑥	Via Postumia (148 B.C.)	⑬	Via Salaria
⑦	Via Valeria		

THE WESTERN MEDITERRANEAN IN 270 B.C.

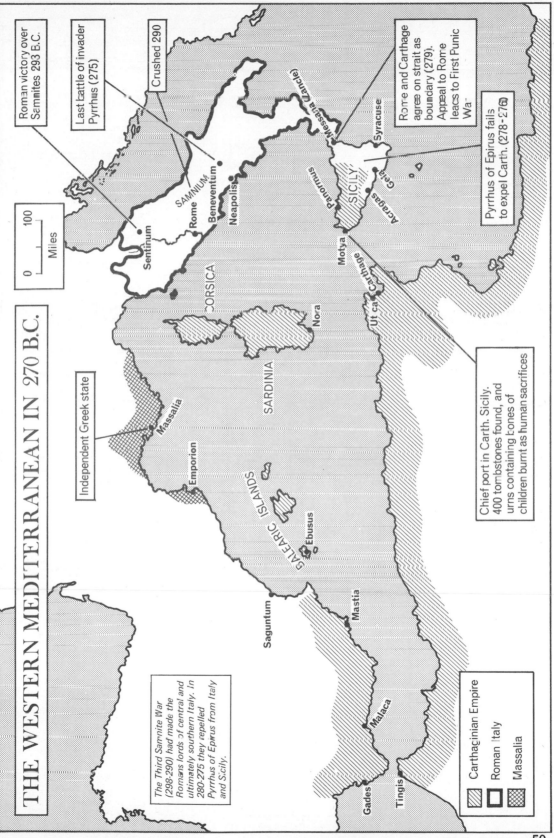

Roman victory over Samnites 293 B.C.

Last battle of invader Pyrrhus (275)

Crushed 290

Rome and Carthage agree on strait as boundary (279). Appeal to Rome leads to First Punic War.

Pyrrhus of Epirus fails to expel Carth. (278-276)

Chief port in Carth. Sicily. 400 tombstones found, and urns containing bones of children burnt as human sacrifices

Independent Greek state

The Third Samnite War (298-290) had made the Romans lords of central and ultimately southern Italy. In 280-275 they repelled Pyrrhus of Epirus from Italy and Sicily.

100

0

Miles

SAMNIUM

Rome
Beneventum
Neapolis
Sentinum

Messana (Zancle)
Syracuse
SICILY
Gela
Acragas
Panormus

CORSICA

Motya
Utica
Carthage

Nora

SARDINIA

Massalia

Emporion

BALEARIC ISLANDS

Ebusus

Saguntum

Mastia

Malaca

Gades
Tingis

Carthaginian Empire

Roman Italy

Massalia

50

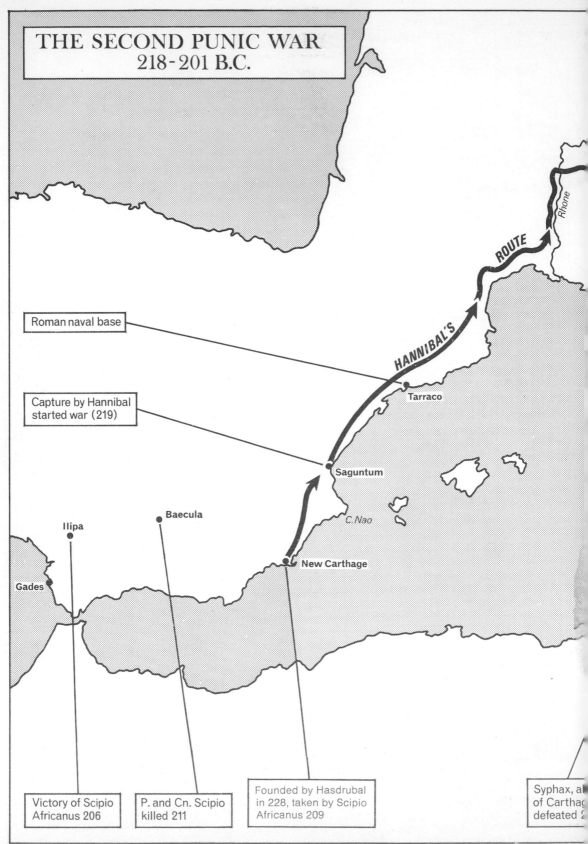

THE SECOND PUNIC WAR
218-201 B.C.

HANNIBAL'S ROUTE

Rhone

Roman naval base

Capture by Hannibal
started war (219)

Tarraco

Saguntum

C. Nao

Baecula

Ilipa

New Carthage

Gades

Victory of Scipio
Africanus 206

P. and Cn. Scipio
killed 211

Founded by Hasdrubal
in 228, taken by Scipio
Africanus 209

Syphax, a
of Carthag
defeated 2

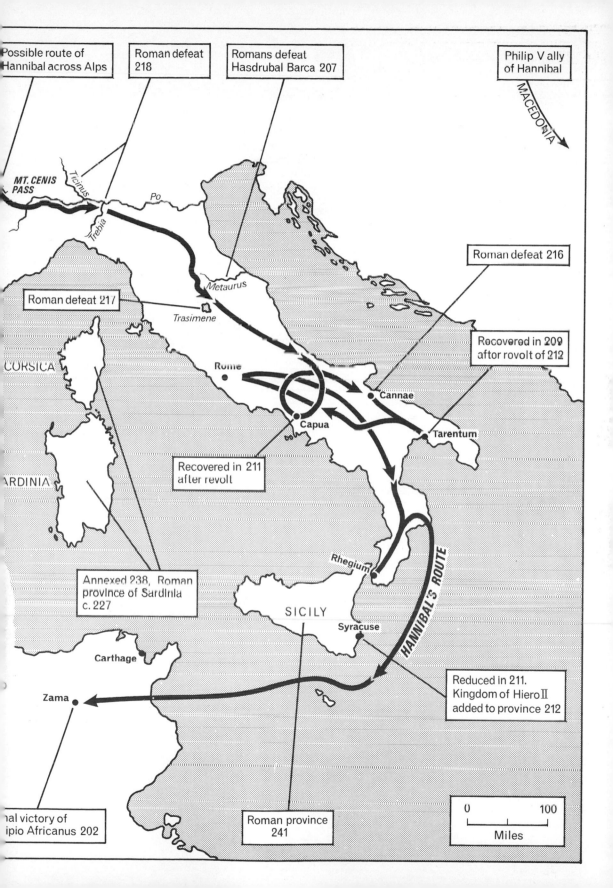

Possible route of
Hannibal across Alps

Roman defeat
218

Romans defeat
Hasdrubal Barca 207

Philip V ally
of Hannibal

MACEDONIA

MT. CENIS
PASS

Ticinus

Po

Trebia

Roman defeat 217

Metaurus

Trasimene

Roman defeat 216

CORSICA

Rome

Recovered in 209
after revolt of 212

Cannae

Capua

Tarentum

Recovered in 211
after revolt

SARDINIA

Annexed 238, Roman
province of Sardinia
c. 227

Rhegium

HANNIBAL'S ROUTE

SICILY

Syracuse

Reduced in 211.
Kingdom of Hiero II
added to province 212

Carthage

Zama

Final victory of
Scipio Africanus 202

Roman province
241

0   100
Miles

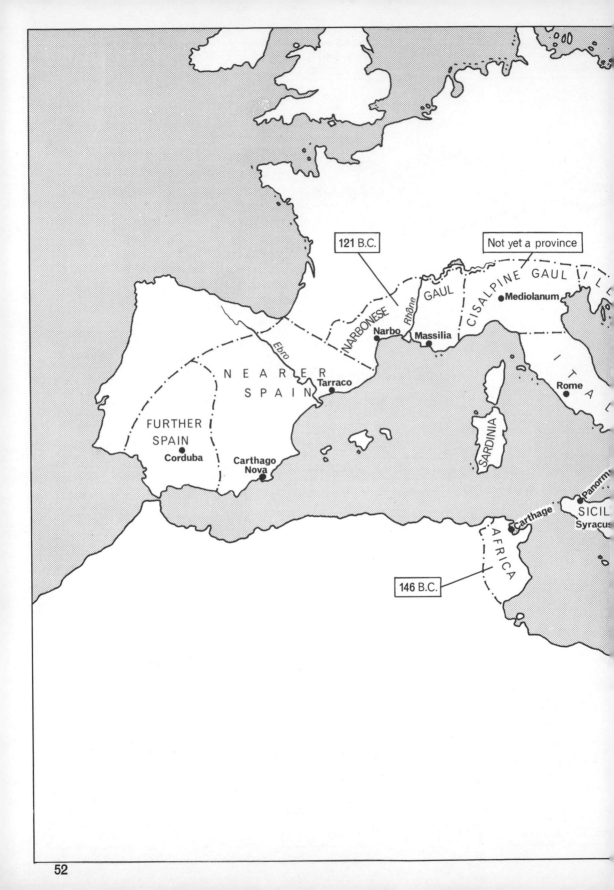

121 B.C.

Not yet a province

GAUL

CISALPINE GAUL

NARBONESE

Rhône

Mediolanum

Narbo

Massilia

Ebro

NEARER
SPAIN

Tarraco

Rome

SARDINIA

FURTHER
SPAIN

Corduba

Carthago
Nova

Panorm

SICIL

Carthage

Syracus

AFRICA

146 B.C.

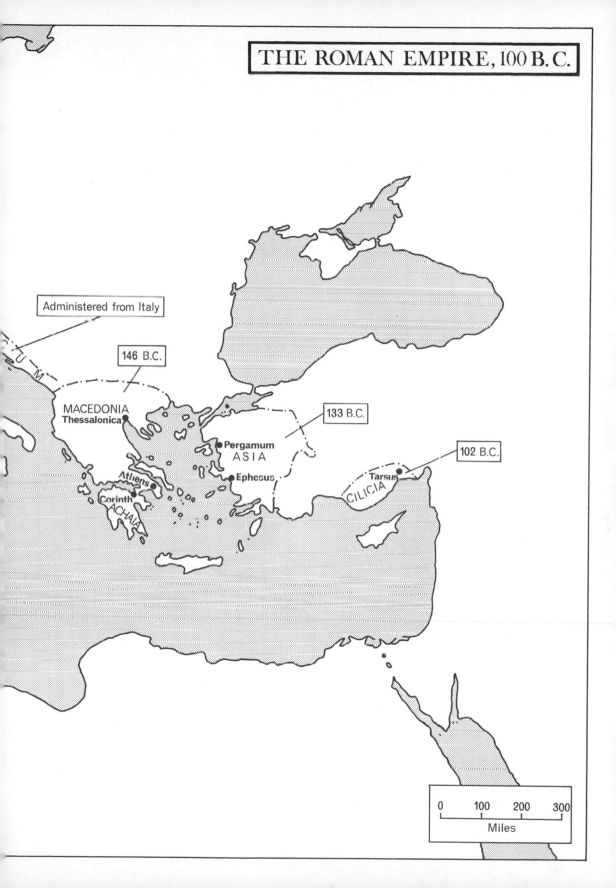

THE ROMAN EMPIRE, 100 B.C.

Administered from Italy

146 B.C.

133 B.C.

102 B.C.

MACEDONIA
Thessalonica

Pergamum
ASIA
Ephesus

Tarsus
CILICIA

Athens

Corinth
ACHAIA

0   100   200   300
Miles

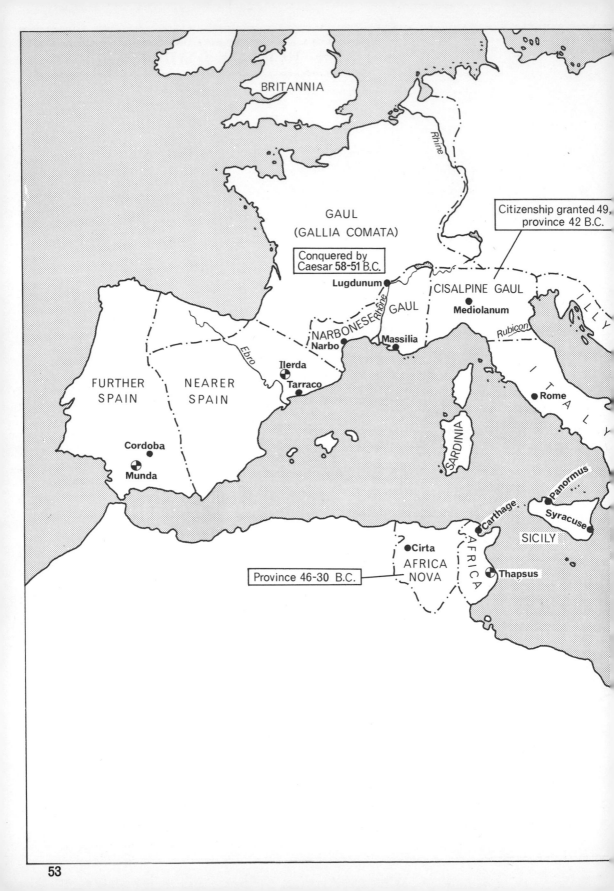

BRITANNIA

GAUL
(GALLIA COMATA)

Conquered by
Caesar 58-51 B.C.

Citizenship granted 49,
province 42 B.C.

Lugdunum

CISALPINE GAUL

Mediolanum

NARBONESE GAUL

Narbo

Massilia

Rubicon

FURTHER
SPAIN

NEARER
SPAIN

Ebro

Ilerda

Tarraco

SARDINIA

Rome

Cordoba

Munda

Carthage

Panormus

Syracuse

SICILY

Cirta

AFRICA
NOVA

AFRICA

Thapsus

Province 46-30 B.C.

Rhine

Rhône

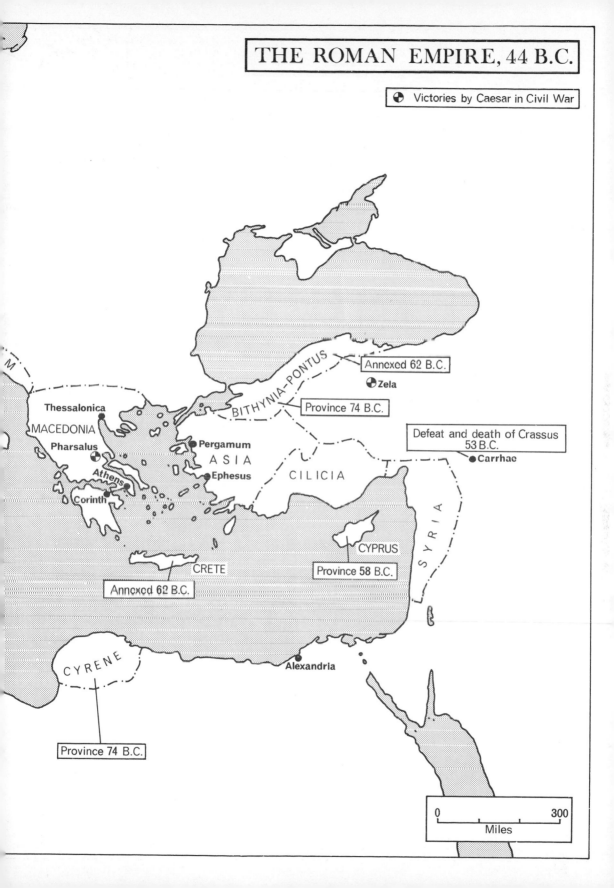

THE ROMAN EMPIRE, 44 B.C.

◑ Victories by Caesar in Civil War

Annexed 62 B.C.

◑ Zela

BITHYNIA-PONTUS

Province 74 B.C.

Defeat and death of Crassus
53 B.C.

● Carrhae

Thessalonica
●

MACEDONIA

Pharsalus
◑

Pergamum ●

A S I A

C I L I C I A

Athens ●
● **Ephesus**

● **Corinth**

S Y R I A

CYPRUS

CRETE

Province 58 B.C.

Annexed 62 B.C.

C Y R E N E

● **Alexandria**

Province 74 B.C.

0		300

Miles

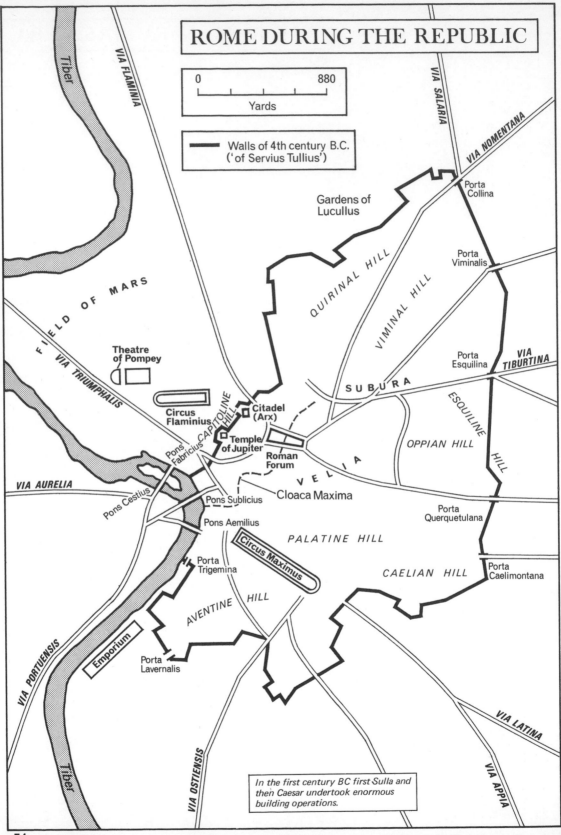

ROME DURING THE REPUBLIC

0 — 880
Yards

━━ Walls of 4th century B.C.
('of Servius Tullius')

Tiber

VIA FLAMINIA

VIA SALARIA

VIA NOMENTANA

Porta
Collina

Gardens of
Lucullus

Porta
Viminalis

QUIRINAL HILL

VIMINAL HILL

FIELD OF MARS

VIA TRIUMPHALIS

Theatre
of Pompey

Porta
Esquilina

*VIA
TIBURTINA*

SUBURA

ESQUILINE

HILL

Circus
Flaminius

CAPITOLINE HILL

Citadel
(Arx)

Temple
of Jupiter

Pons
Fabricius

Roman
Forum

VELIA

OPPIAN HILL

VIA AURELIA

Pons Cestius

Pons Sublicius

Cloaca Maxima

Pons Aemilius

Porta
Querquetulana

PALATINE HILL

Circus Maximus

Porta
Trigemina

CAELIAN HILL

Porta
Caelimontana

AVENTINE HILL

Emporium

VIA PORTUENSIS

Porta
Lavernalis

Tiber

VIA OSTIENSIS

VIA LATINA

VIA APPIA

*In the first century BC first Sulla and
then Caesar undertook enormous
building operations.*

54

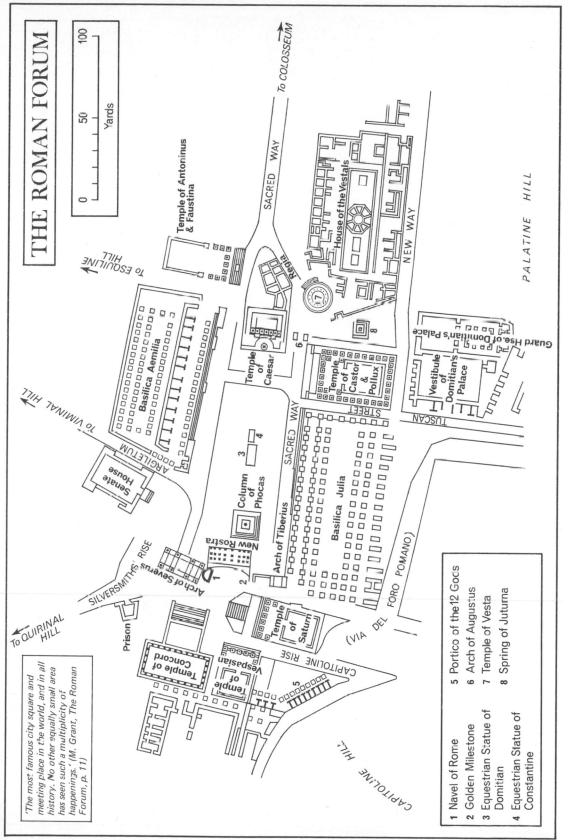

THE ROMAN FORUM

Yards
0   50   100

To ESQUILINE HILL

Temple of Antoninus & Faustina

SACRED WAY

To COLOSSEUM

Regia

House of the Vestals

7

NEW WAY

PALATINE HILL

To VIMINAL HILL

Basilica Aemilia

ARGILETUM

Senate House

Temple of Caesar

8

Guard Hse. of Domitian's Palace

6

Temple of Castor & Pollux

STREET

Vestibule of Domitian's Palace

TUSCAN

SACRED WAY

Column of Phocas

3
4

New Rostra

Arch of Tiberius

Basilica Julia

To QUIRINAL HILL

SILVERSMITH'S RISE

Arch of Severus

2
1

Prison

Temple of Concord

Temple of Vesasian

Temple of Saturn

CAPITOLINE RISE

5

(VIA DEL FORO ROMANO)

CAPITOLINE HILL

'The most famous city square and meeting place in the world, and in all history. No other equally small area has seen such a multiplicity of happenings.' (M. Grant, *The Roman Forum*, p. 11)

1 Navel of Rome
2 Golden Milestone
3 Equestrian Statue of Domitian
4 Equestrian Statue of Constantine
5 Portico of the 12 Gods
6 Arch of Augustus
7 Temple of Vesta
8 Spring of Juturna

55

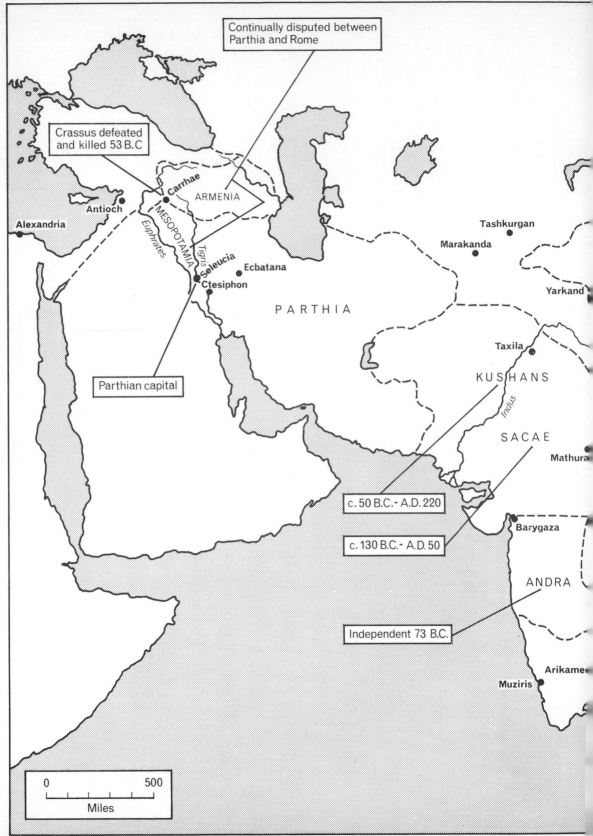

Continually disputed between
Parthia and Rome

Crassus defeated
and killed 53 B.C

Carrhae

ARMENIA

Antioch

Alexandria

MESOPOTAMIA

Euphrates

Tigris

Seleucia

Ecbatana

Ctesiphon

PARTHIA

Parthian capital

Tashkurgan

Marakanda

Yarkand

Taxila

KUSHANS

Indus

SACAE

Mathura

c. 50 B.C. - A.D. 220

c. 130 B.C. - A.D. 50

Barygaza

ANDRA

Independent 73 B.C.

Arikame

Muziris

0   500
Miles

PARTHIA AND THE EAST

HSIUNG-NU

KASHGARIA

Chinese c 100 B.C.- 9 A.D. and from 60 A.D.

Capital of Earlier (Western) Han 202 B.C.

Capital of Later (Eastern) Han A.D. 23

Hwang-ho

Loyang

Ch'ang-an (Sian)

Yangtse

CHINA

Pataliputra (Patna)

Ganges

MAGHADA

LINGA

Daluro

Independent 157 B.C.

The Parthian Empire, the only major power on Rome's frontiers, was a loose feudal structure created by the Arsacid dynasty in c 248-7 BC. It was overthrown by the Sassanian Persians in AD 223-6. The capital of both empires was Ctesiphon, across the Tigris from the Greek city of Seleucia.

BRITANNIA

FREE GERMANY

LWR. GERMANY (17 B.C.)

Temporarily conquered from 15 B.C. but abandoned after ambushing of Varus by Arminius in A.D. 9

Colonia Agrippinensis

BELGICA

Rhine

Moguntiacum

Danube

LOWER PANNONIA (10 B.C.)

LUGDUNENSIS

UPR. GERMANY (17 B.C.)

RHAETIA (15 B.C.)

NORICUM (15 B.C.)

UPPER PANNONIA

P

Aquileia

Lugdunum

AQUITANIA

C

M

I T A L Y

Adriatic Sea

NARBONENSIS

Nemausus

Rome

TARRACONENSIS

Tarraco

LUSITANIA (c. 27 B.C.)

Corduba

BAETICA

Naulochus

SICILY

Gades

Carthage

MAURETANIA

Naval victory over Sextus Pompeius 36 B.C.

A F R I C A

—————— Imperial frontier as in A.D. 14

– – – – Provincial frontiers

<u>ASIA</u> Senatorial provinces

<u>ALPINE PROVINCES</u> (15 - 14 B.C.)
M: Maritime, C: Cottian, P: Pennine

The hatched areas represent the more important dependent ('client') states, whose monarchs enjoyed internal autonomy but had to support Rome's foreign policy and help defend the imperial frontiers.

///// Principal client states

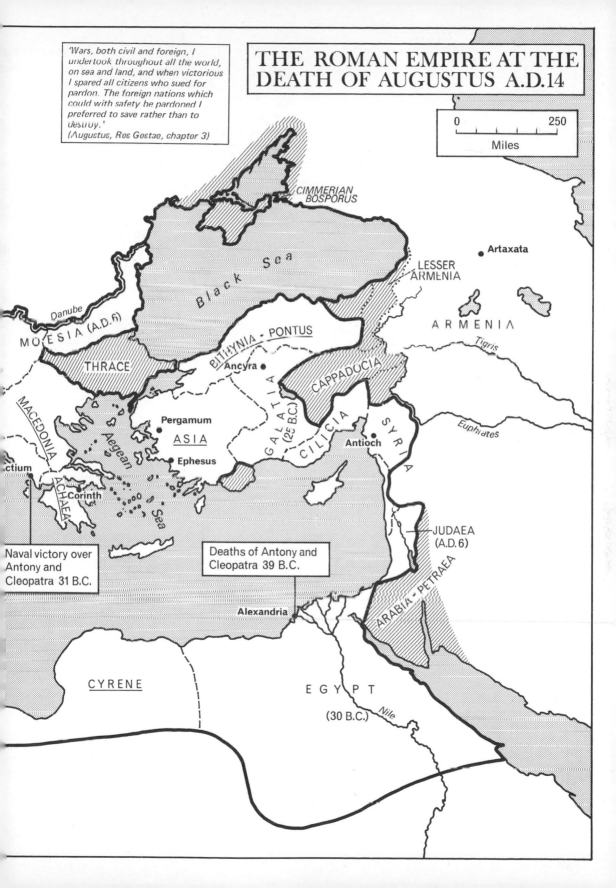

THE ROMAN EMPIRE AT THE
DEATH OF AUGUSTUS A.D.14

'Wars, both civil and foreign, I
undertook throughout all the world,
on sea and land, and when victorious
I spared all citizens who sued for
pardon. The foreign nations which
could with safety be pardoned I
preferred to save rather than to
destroy.'
(Augustus, Res Gestae, chapter 3)

0   250
Miles

CIMMERIAN
BOSPORUS

• Artaxata

LESSER
ARMENIA

Black Sea

A R M E N I A

Danube

Tigris

MOESIA (A.D.6)

BITHYNIA - PONTUS

THRACE

Ancyra •

CAPPADOCIA

GALATIA
(25 B.C.)

CILICIA

SYRIA

Euphrates

MACEDONIA

Pergamum
•

ASIA

Antioch •

Ephesus
•

ctium

Aegean Sea

ACHAEA

• Corinth

JUDAEA
(A.D.6)

Naval victory over
Antony and
Cleopatra 31 B.C.

Deaths of Antony and
Cleopatra 39 B.C.

ARABIA - PETRAEA

Alexandria •

CYRENE

E G Y P T

(30 B.C.)

Nile

GAUL

Rhine

Danube

Adriatic Sea

Rhone

Arelate

VIA DOMITIA

Narbo

Forum Julii

Ebro

Rome

SPAIN

Tyrrhenian Sea

Mediterranean

AFRICA

Imperial frontier as in A.D. 14

Roman roads

Mountain contours

All roads lead to Rome: the most potent guarantees of external and internal peace and stimulants of prosperity.

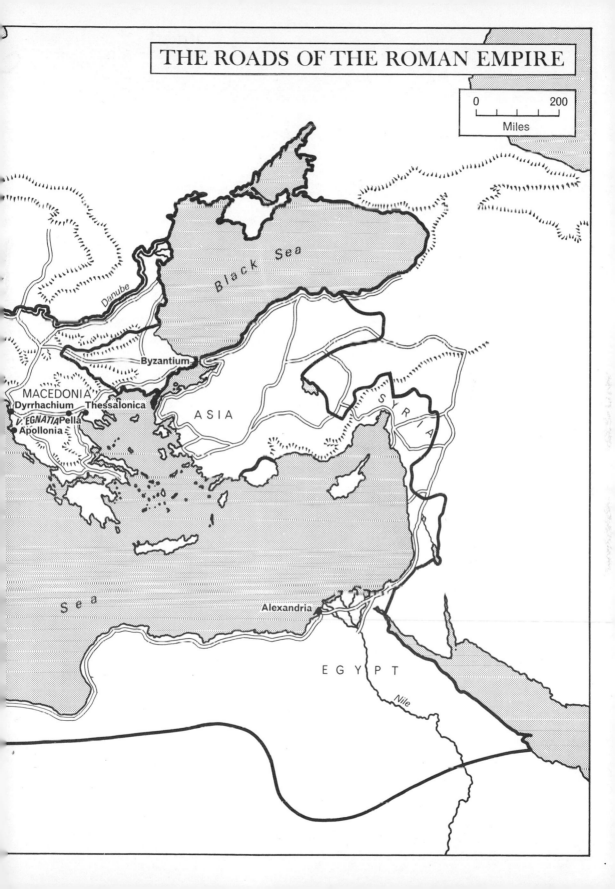

THE ROADS OF THE ROMAN EMPIRE

0   200
Miles

Black Sea

Danube

Byzantium

MACEDONIA
Dyrrhachium   **Thessalonica**
*V. EGNATIA***Pella**
Apollonia

ASIA

S Y R I A

Sea

Alexandria

E G Y P T

Nile

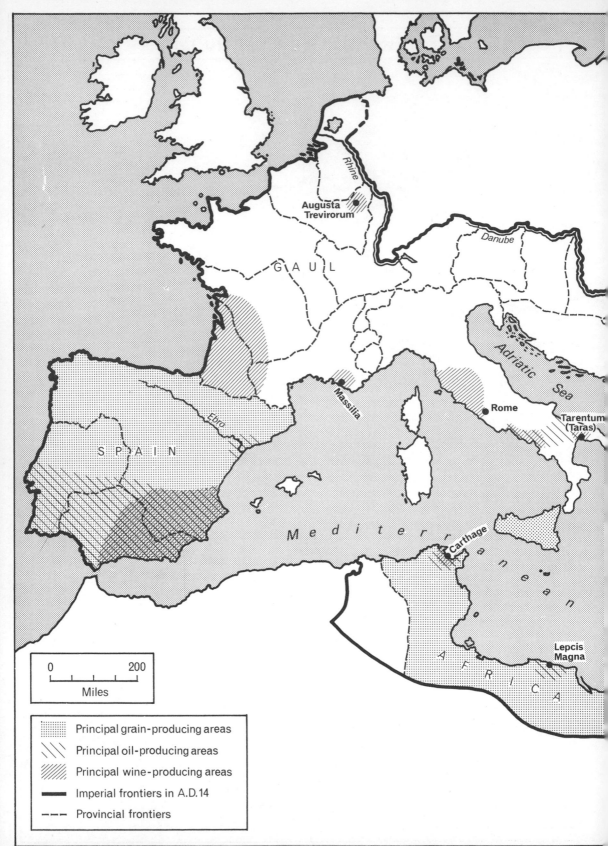

Augusta
Trevirorum

Rhine

Danube

G A U L

Adriatic Sea

Ebro

Massilia

Rome

Tarentum
(Taras)

S P A I N

M e d i t e r r a n e a n

Carthage

A F R I C A

Lepcis
Magna

0   200
Miles

Principal grain-producing areas

Principal oil-producing areas

Principal wine-producing areas

Imperial frontiers in A.D. 14

Provincial frontiers

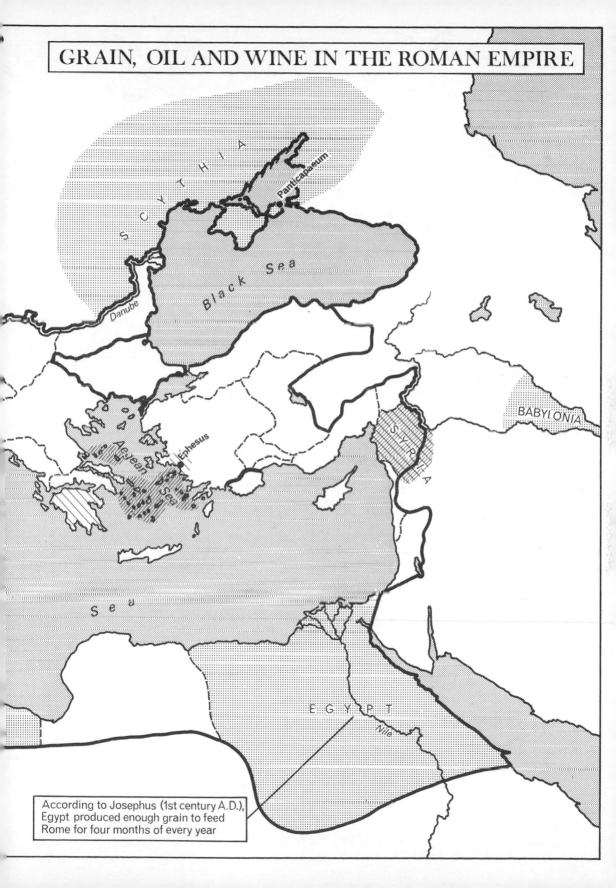

GRAIN, OIL AND WINE IN THE ROMAN EMPIRE

SCYTHIA

Panticapaeum

Black Sea

Danube

BABYLONIA

SYRIA

Aegean Sea

Ephesus

Sea

EGYPT

Nile

According to Josephus (1st century A.D.), Egypt produced enough grain to feed Rome for four months of every year

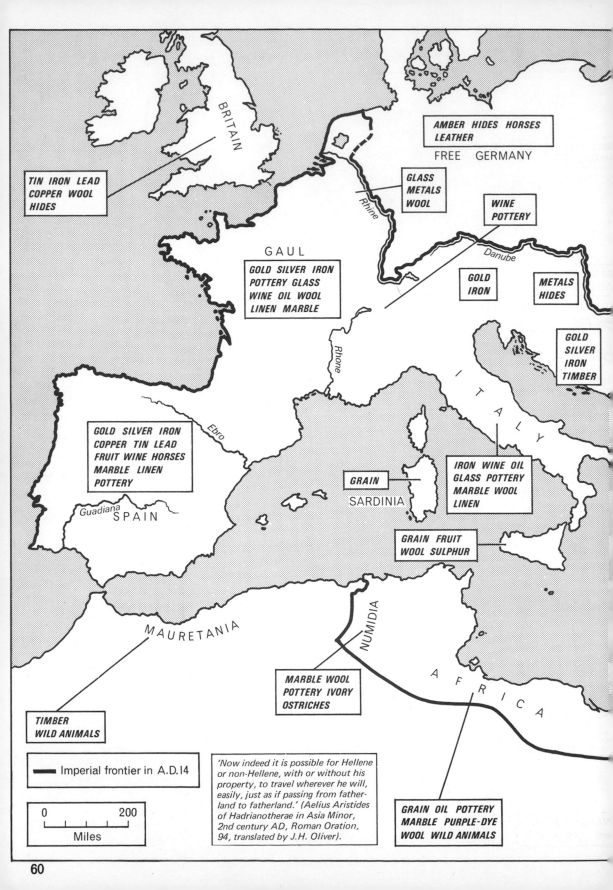

BRITAIN

TIN IRON LEAD
COPPER WOOL
HIDES

AMBER HIDES HORSES
LEATHER

FREE GERMANY

GLASS
METALS
WOOL

Rhine

WINE
POTTERY

GAUL

GOLD SILVER IRON
POTTERY GLASS
WINE OIL WOOL
LINEN MARBLE

Danube

GOLD
IRON

METALS
HIDES

Rhone

GOLD
SILVER
IRON
TIMBER

ITALY

GOLD SILVER IRON
COPPER TIN LEAD
FRUIT WINE HORSES
MARBLE LINEN
POTTERY

Ebro

GRAIN

SARDINIA

IRON WINE OIL
GLASS POTTERY
MARBLE WOOL
LINEN

Guadiana SPAIN

GRAIN FRUIT
WOOL SULPHUR

MAURETANIA

NUMIDIA

AFRICA

MARBLE WOOL
POTTERY IVORY
OSTRICHES

TIMBER
WILD ANIMALS

Imperial frontier in A.D.14

| 0 | | | 200 |

Miles

'Now indeed it is possible for Hellene
or non-Hellene, with or without his
property, to travel wherever he will,
easily, just as if passing from fatherland to fatherland.' (Aelius Aristides
of Hadrianotherae in Asia Minor,
2nd century AD, Roman Oration,
94, translated by J.H. Oliver).

GRAIN OIL POTTERY
MARBLE PURPLE-DYE
WOOL WILD ANIMALS

60

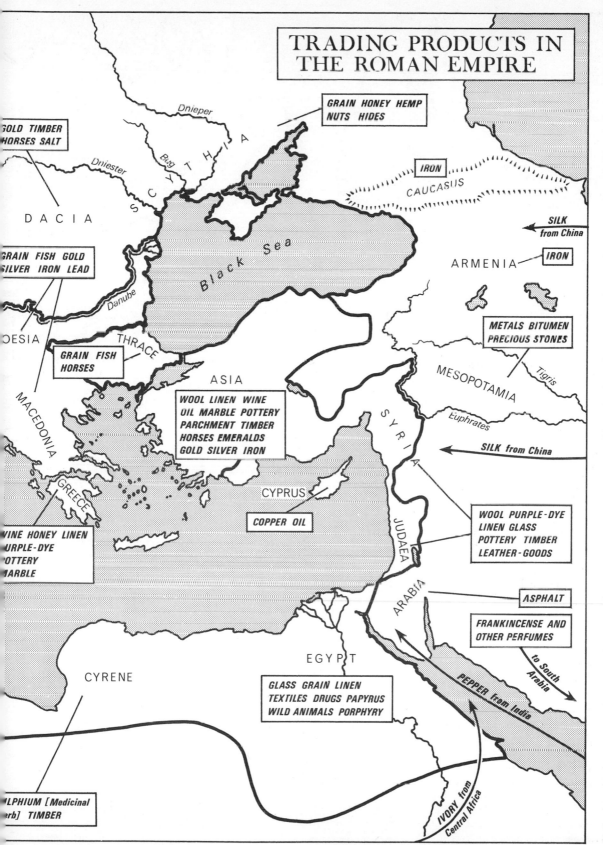

TRADING PRODUCTS IN THE ROMAN EMPIRE

Dnieper

GOLD TIMBER
HORSES SALT

Dniester

Bug

S C Y T H I A

GRAIN HONEY HEMP
NUTS HIDES

IRON

CAUCASUS

SILK
from China

D A C I A

Black Sea

ARMENIA — IRON

GRAIN FISH GOLD
SILVER IRON LEAD

Danube

METALS BITUMEN
PRECIOUS STONES

OESIA

THRACE

MESOPOTAMIA

Tigris

GRAIN FISH
HORSES

ASIA

WOOL LINEN WINE
OIL MARBLE POTTERY
PARCHMENT TIMBER
HORSES EMERALDS
GOLD SILVER IRON

S Y R I A

Euphrates

SILK from China

MACEDONIA

GREECE

CYPRUS

COPPER OIL

WOOL PURPLE-DYE
LINEN GLASS
POTTERY TIMBER
LEATHER-GOODS

JUDAEA

WINE HONEY LINEN
PURPLE-DYE
POTTERY
MARBLE

ARABIA

ASPHALT

FRANKINCENSE AND
OTHER PERFUMES

to South Arabia

EGYPT

GLASS GRAIN LINEN
TEXTILES DRUGS PAPYRUS
WILD ANIMALS PORPHYRY

PEPPER from India

CYRENE

IVORY from
Central Africa

LPHIUM [Medicinal
erb] TIMBER

Major mints. Date at which Rome supersedes Lugdunum uncertain. Designs of copper, and perhaps for a time silver coins, imitated at many other mints.

BELGICA

LUGDUNENSIS

GAUL

RHAETIA

NORICUM

ILLYRICUM

Extensive bronze city-coinages cease under Caligula (A.D. 37 - 41)

AQUITANIA

Lugdunum ♦ □ ■ ▲

NARBONENSIS

Nemausus ○

I T A L Y

Rome ■ ▲ □ ♦

Large temporary city-coinage circulates through-out west

TARRACONENSIS

S P A I N ○

LUSITANIA

BAETICA

NUMIDIA

A F R I C A ○

■	Gold
▲	Silver
△	Base silver
□	Brass
○	Bronze
♦	Copper

<u>Note</u>: Augustus reformed and enlarged the Roman imperial coinage, issuing gold, silver, brass and copper on an enormous scale

Small bronze city-coinages virtually cease under Tiberius (A.D. 14)

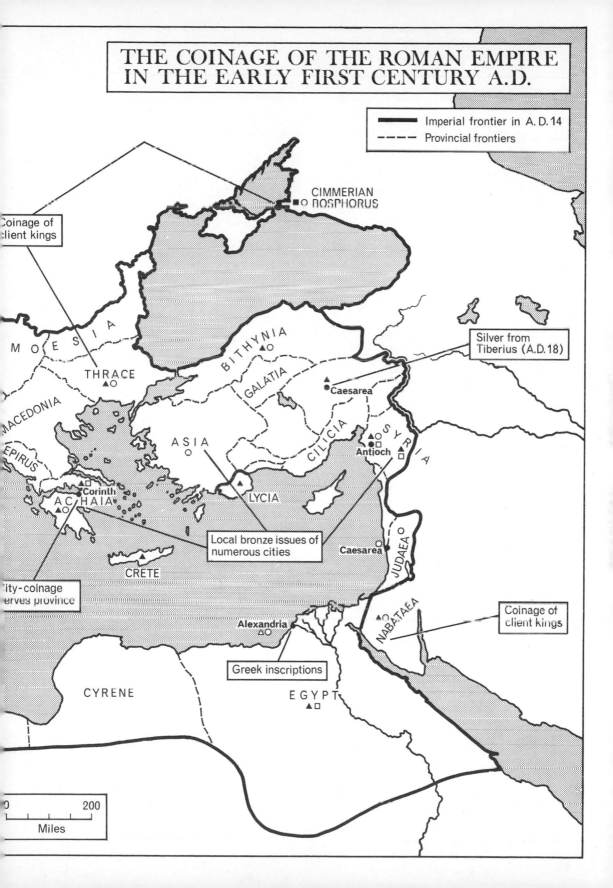

THE COINAGE OF THE ROMAN EMPIRE
IN THE EARLY FIRST CENTURY A.D.

Imperial frontier in A.D.14
Provincial frontiers

Coinage of
client kings

CIMMERIAN
BOSPHORUS

Silver from
Tiberius (A.D.18)

M O E S I A

THRACE

BITHYNIA

GALATIA

Caesarea

MACEDONIA

ASIA

CILICIA

SYRIA

Antioch

EPIRUS

Corinth

ACHAIA

LYCIA

Local bronze issues of
numerous cities

Caesarea

JUDAEA

CRETE

City-coinage
serves province

NABATAEA

Coinage of
client kings

Alexandria

Greek inscriptions

CYRENE

E G Y P T

0   200
Miles

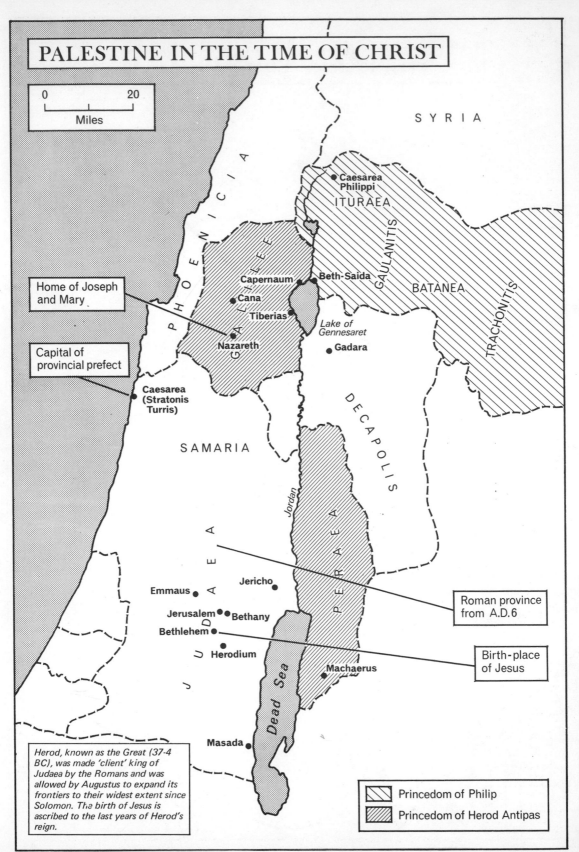

PALESTINE IN THE TIME OF CHRIST

0   20
Miles

SYRIA

P H O E N I C I A

Caesarea
Philippi

ITURAEA

G A U L A N I T I S

BATANEA

T R A C H O N I T I S

Capernaum
Cana

Beth-Saida

Home of Joseph
and Mary

Tiberias

Nazareth

Lake of
Gennesaret

Gadara

D E C A P O L I S

Capital of
provincial prefect

Caesarea
(Stratonis
Turris)

SAMARIA

Jordan

J U D A E A

P E R A E A

Jericho

Emmaus

Jerusalem ● ● Bethany

Bethlehem ●

Herodium

Dead Sea

Machaerus

Roman province
from A.D. 6

Birth-place
of Jesus

Masada

Herod, known as the Great (37-4
BC), was made 'client' king of
Judaea by the Romans and was
allowed by Augustus to expand its
frontiers to their widest extent since
Solomon. The birth of Jesus is
ascribed to the last years of Herod's
reign.

Princedom of Philip

Princedom of Herod Antipas

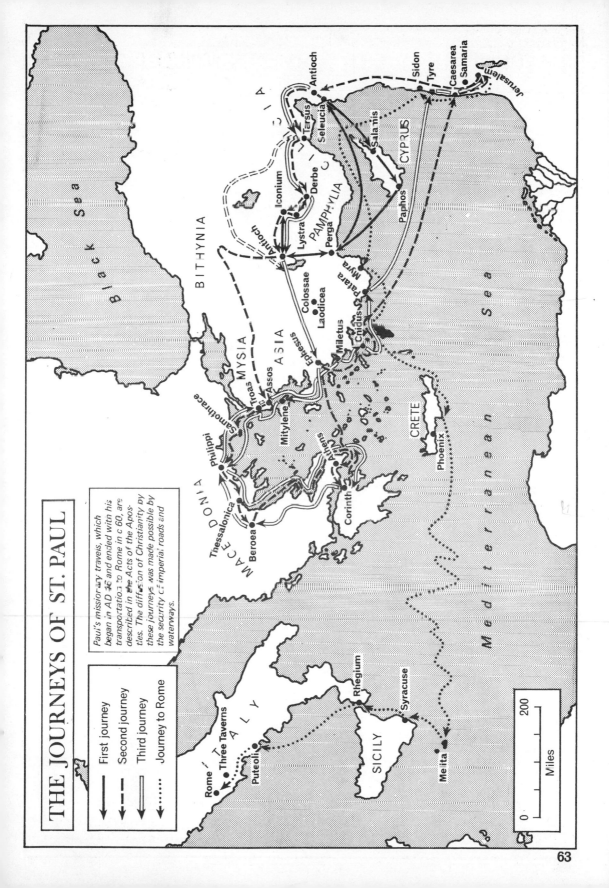

THE JOURNEYS OF ST. PAUL

Legend:
- First journey
- Second journey
- Third journey
- Journey to Rome

Paul's missionary travels, which began in AD 46 and ended with his transportation to Rome in c 60, are described in the Acts of the Apostles. The diffusion of Christianity by these journeys was made possible by the security of imperial roads and waterways.

Black Sea

BITHYNIA

Antioch
Tarsus
Seleucia
Salamis
CYPRUS
Sidon
Tyre
Caesarea
Samaria
Jerusalem
Paphos
Iconium
Derbe
Lystra
Antioch
PAMPHYLIA
Perga
Myra
Patara
Colossae
Laodicea
Cnidus
Miletus
Ephesus
MYSIA
ASIA
Troas
Assos
Samothrace
Mitylene
Philippi
Athens
CRETE
Phoenix
MACEDONIA
Thessalonica
Beroea
Corinth

Mediterranean Sea

ITALY
Rome
Three Taverns
Puteoli
Rhegium
Syracuse
SICILY
Melita

Scale:
Miles
0 — 200

63

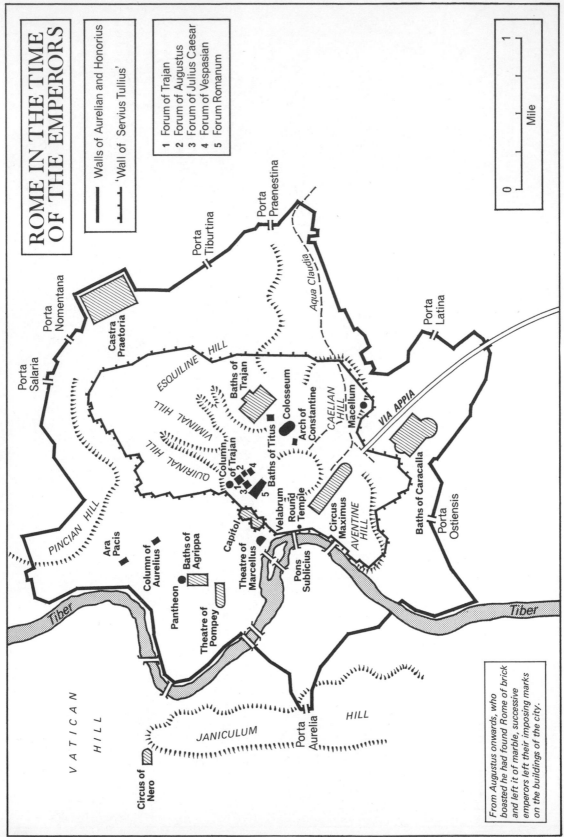

ROME IN THE TIME OF THE EMPERORS

Walls of Aurelian and Honorius
'Wall of Servius Tullius'

1 Forum of Trajan
2 Forum of Augustus
3 Forum of Julius Caesar
4 Forum of Vespasian
5 Forum Romanum

0 — Mile — 1

Porta Praenestina
Porta Tiburtina
Porta Nomentana
Castra Praetoria
Porta Salaria
ESQUILINE HILL
Baths of Trajan
Colosseum
Aqua Claudia
Porta Latina
CAELIAN HILL
Macellum
VIA APPIA
VIMINAL HILL
Arch of Constantine
Baths of Titus
QUIRINAL HILL
Column of Trajan
1 2 4
3 5
Velabrum
Round Temple
Circus Maximus
Baths of Caracalla
AVENTINE HILL
Porta Ostiensis
PINCIAN HILL
Ara Pacis
Column of Aurelius
Baths of Agrippa
Capitol
Theatre of Marcellus
Pons Sublicius
Pantheon
Theatre of Pompey
Tiber
Tiber
VATICAN HILL
JANICULUM HILL
Porta Aurelia
Circus of Nero

From Augustus onwards, who boasted he had found Rome of brick and left it of marble, successive emperors left their imposing marks on the buildings of the city.

64

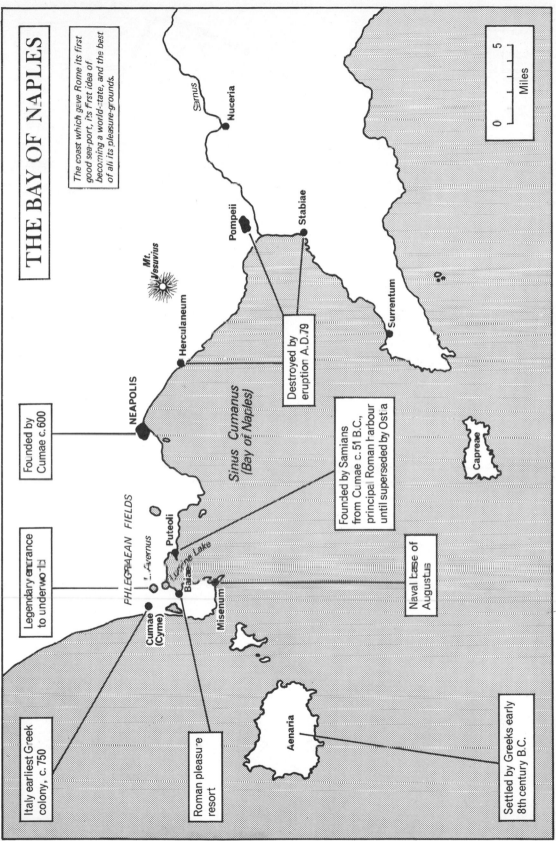

THE BAY OF NAPLES

The coast which gave Rome its first good sea-port, its first idea of becoming a world-state, and the best of all its pleasure-grounds.

Sarnus

Nuceria

Pompeii

Stabiae

Mt. Vesuvius

Herculaneum

Surrentum

Destroyed by eruption A.D.79

NEAPOLIS

Founded by Cumae c.600

Sinus Cumanus
(Bay of Naples)

Founded by Samians from Cumae c. 51 B.C., principal Roman harbour until superseded by Ostia

Capreae

Legendary entrance to underworld

Puteoli

PHLEGRAEAN FIELDS

L. Avernus

Lucrine Lake

Naval base of Augustus

Baiae

Misenum

Cumae (Cyme)

Italy's earliest Greek colony, c. 750

Roman pleasure resort

Aenaria

Settled by Greeks early 8th century B.C.

0 5 Miles

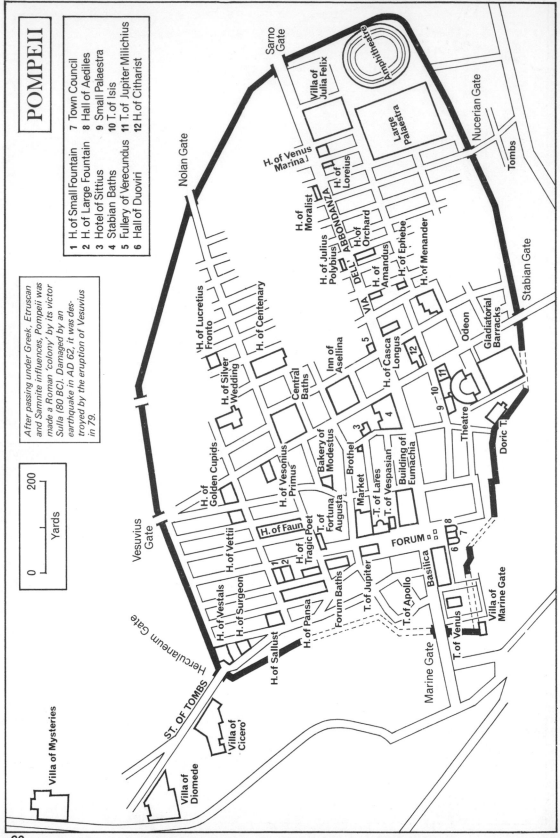

POMPEII

1 H. of Small Fountain
2 H. of Large Fountain
3 Hotel of Sittius
4 Stabian Baths
5 Fullery of Verecundus
6 Hall of Duoviri
7 Town Council
8 Hall of Aediles
9 Small Palaestra
10 T. of Isis
11 T. of Jupiter Milichius
12 H. of Citharist

After passing under Greek, Etruscan and Samnite influences, Pompeii was made a Roman 'colony' by its victor Sulla (80 BC). Damaged by an earthquake in AD 62, it was destroyed by the eruption of Vesuvius in 79.

Yards
0   200

Villa of Mysteries
Villa of Diomede
'Villa of Cicero'
ST. OF TOMBS
Herculaneum Gate
H. of Sallust
H. of Vestals
H. of Surgeon
H. of Pansa
Forum Baths
H. of Vettii
H. of Faun
H. of Tragic Poet
H. of Golden Cupids
H. of Silver Wedding
H. of Vesonius Primus
Bakery of Modestus
H. of Centenary
H. of Lucretius Fronto
Vesuvius Gate
Nolan Gate
T. of Fortuna Augusta
T. of Jupiter
T. of Apollo
Basilica
FORUM
Market
T. of Lares
T. of Vespasian
Building of Eumachia
Brothel
Central Baths
Inn of Asellina
H. of Casca Longus
VIA DELL' ABBONDANZA
H. of Julius Polybius
H. of Orchard
H. of Amandus
H. of Ephebe
H. of Menander
H. of Moralist
H. of Venus Marina
Villa of Julia Felix
Large Palaestra
Amphitheatre
Sarno Gate
Nucerian Gate
Tombs
Stabian Gate
Odeon
Gladiatorial Barracks
Theatre
Doric T.
H. of Loreius
T. of Venus
Villa of Marine Gate
Marine Gate

66

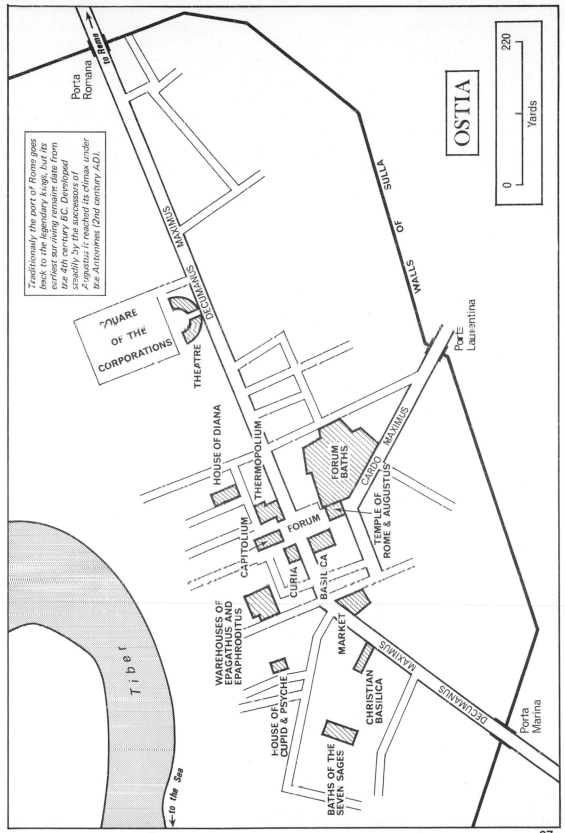

OSTIA

Traditionally the port of Rome goes back to the legendary kings, but its earliest surviving remains date from the 4th century BC. Developed steadily by the successors of Augustus it reached its climax under the Antonines (2nd century AD).

0   220
Yards

to Rome
Porta Romana

WALLS   OF   SULLA

Porta Laurentina

DECUMANUS   MAXIMUS

SQUARE OF THE CORPORATIONS

THEATRE

HOUSE OF DIANA

THERMOPOLIUM

FORUM BATHS

CAPITOLIUM

FORUM

CARDO   MAXIMUS

TEMPLE OF ROME & AUGUSTUS

CURIA

BASILICA

WAREHOUSES OF EPAGATHUS AND EPAPHRODITUS

Tiber

to the Sea

MARKET

HOUSE OF CUPID & PSYCHE

CHRISTIAN BASILICA

BATHS OF THE SEVEN SAGES

DECUMANUS   MAXIMUS

Porta Marina

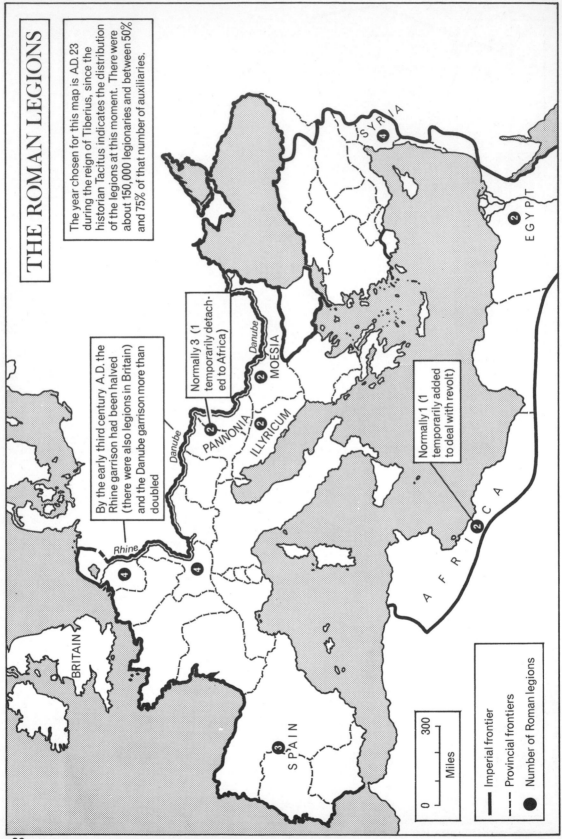

THE ROMAN LEGIONS

The year chosen for this map is A.D. 23 during the reign of Tiberius, since the historian Tacitus indicates the distribution of the legions at this moment. There were about 150,000 legionaries and between 50% and 75% of that number of auxiliaries.

By the early third century A.D. the Rhine garrison had been halved (there were also legions in Britain) and the Danube garrison more than doubled

Normally 3 (1 temporarily detached to Africa)

Normally 1 (1 temporarily added to deal with revolt)

SYRIA ④

EGYPT ②

Danube

MOESIA ②

PANNONIA ②

ILLYRICUM ②

Danube

Rhine

BRITAIN

④ ④

SPAIN ③

A F R I C A ②

Imperial frontier
Provincial frontiers
● Number of Roman legions

0   300
Miles

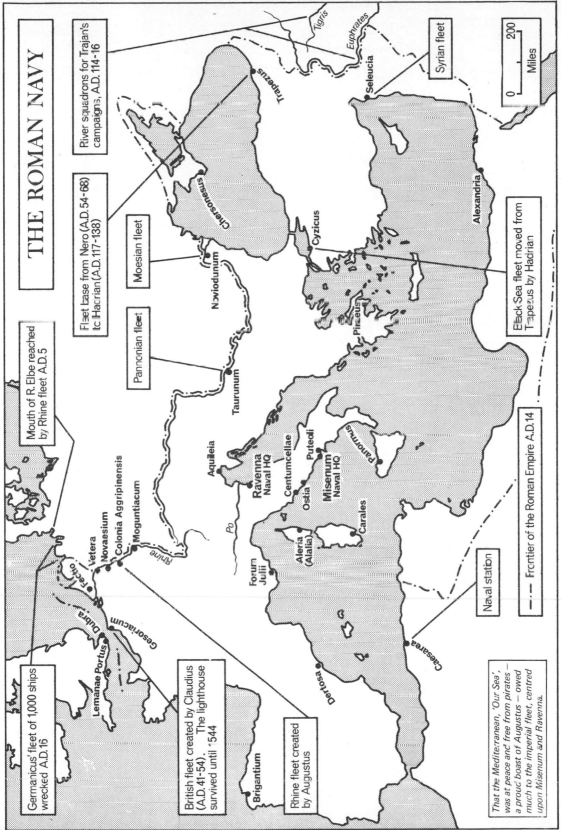

THE ROMAN NAVY

River squadrons for Trajan's campaigns, A.D. 114-16

Fleet base from Nero (A.D. 54-68) to Hadrian (A.D. 117-138)

Moesian fleet

Pannonian fleet

Syrian fleet

Black Sea fleet moved from Trapezus by Hadrian

Mouth of R. Elbe reached by Rhine fleet A.D. 5

Germanicus' fleet of 1,000 ships wrecked A.D. 16

British fleet created by Claudius (A.D. 41-54). The lighthouse survived until ˜544

Rhine fleet created by Augustus

Naval station

− · − · − Frontier of the Roman Empire A.D. 14

That the Mediterranean, 'Our Sea', was at peace and free from pirates — a proud boast of Augustus — owed much to the imperial fleet, centred upon Misenum and Ravenna.

Tigris

Euphrates

Seleucia

Trapezus

Alexandria

Chersonesus

Cyzicus

Istrus

Noviodunum

Piraeus

Taurunum

Aquileia

Ravenna Naval HQ

Centumcellae

Puteoli

Ostia

Misenum Naval HQ

Panormus

Carales

Forum Julii

Aleria (Alalia)

Po

Vetera

Novaesium

Colonia Agrippinensis

Moguntiacum

Rhine

Fectio

Dubris

Gesoriacum

Lemanae Portus

Brigantium

Caesarea

Dertosa

200

0

Miles

69

BRITANNIA (AD 71)
(AD 59)
(AD 43-47)
Londinium

FREE GERMANY

LOWER GERMANY
Colonia Agrippinensis

Moguntiacum

Rhine

AGRI DECUMAT. (83)

RHAETIA

NORICUM

PANNONIA UPPER

Danube

LOWER

LUGDUNENSIS

UPPER GERMANY

G A L L I A

Lugdunum

AQUITANIA

NARBONENSIS

Nemausus

Aquileia

ILLYRICUM

Adriatic Sea

I T A L I A

TARRACONENSIS

H I S P A N I A

Tarraco

Rome

LUSITANIA

SARDINIA

BAETICA

Corduba

Gades

SICILY

Carthage

MAURETANIA (A.D. 42)

A F R I C A

- - - Frontier of Roman Empire A.D. 14
- · - Frontier of Roman Empire A.D. 117
····· Province boundaries

70

THE ROMAN EMPIRE FROM TIBERIUS (A.D.14-37) TO TRAJAN (98-117)

Trajan's expansion as far as the Persian Gulf came to nothing, since his successor Hadrian withdrew to the Euphrates again.

KINGDOM OF BOSPHORUS

Black Sea

Artaxata

ARMENIA MINOR (63)

ARMENIA (A.D.114)

ESIA

THRACIA (A.D.44)

BITHYNIA - PONTUS

Ancyra

CAPPADOCIA (A.D.17)

ASSYRIA (A.D.115)

GALATIA

Pergamum

ASIA

MESOPOTAMIA (A.D.115)

Tigris

Aegean Sea

PAMPHYLIA (43)

Antioch

Corinth

Ephesus

LYCIA

S Y R I A

Euphrates

JUDAEA (A.D.6,44)

Alexandria

ARABIA (A.D.106)

CYRENE

Regions beyond Euphrates evacuated by Hadrian A.D.117

E G Y P T

Nile

0   200
Miles

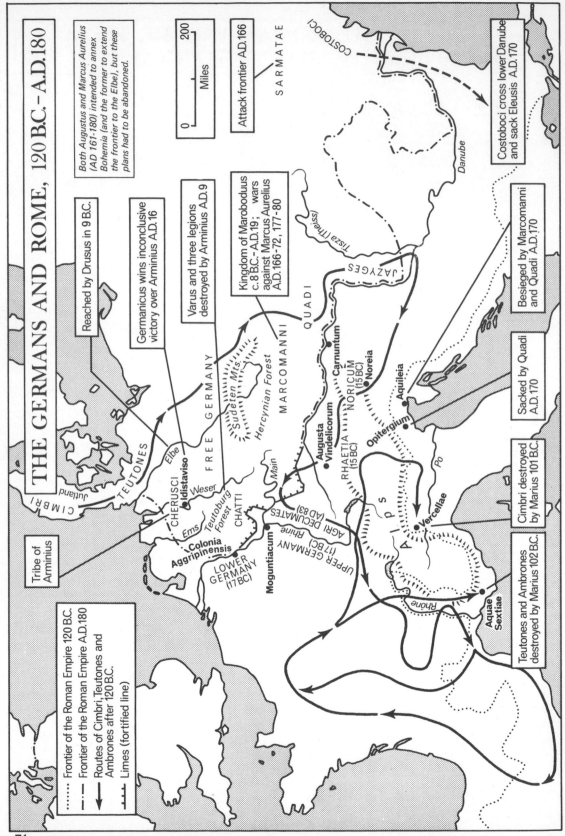

THE GERMANS AND ROME, 120 B.C.–A.D.180

Both Augustus and Marcus Aurelius (AD 161-180) intended to annex Bohemia (and the former to extend the frontier to the Elbe), but these plans had to be abandoned.

Reached by Drusus in 9 B.C.

Germanicus wins inconclusive victory over Arminius A.D.16

Varus and three legions destroyed by Arminius A.D.9

Kingdom of Maroboduus c.8 B.C.–A.D.19; wars against Marcus Aurelius A.D.166-72, 177-80

Attack frontier A.D.166

Costoboci cross lower Danube and sack Eleusis A.D.170

Besieged by Marcomanni and Quadi A.D.170

Sacked by Quadi A.D.170

Cimbri destroyed by Marius 101 B.C.

Teutones and Ambrones destroyed by Marius 102 B.C.

Tribe of Arminius

....	Frontier of the Roman Empire 120 B.C.
–·–·–	Frontier of the Roman Empire A.D.180
→→	Routes of Cimbri, Teutones and Ambrones after 120 B.C.
⊥⊥⊥	Limes (fortified line)

200 Miles

SARMATAE
COSTOBOCI
Danube
Tisza (Theiss)
JAZYGES
QUADI
MARCOMANNI
Hercynian Forest
Sudeten Mts.
FREE GERMANY
TEUTONES
CIMBRI
Jutland
Elbe
CHERUSCI ● Idistaviso
Weser
Ems
Teutoburg Forest
CHATTI
Main
● Colonia Agripinensis
LOWER GERMANY (17BC)
● Moguntiacum
Rhine
UPPER GERMANY (17BC)
AGRI DECUMATES (AD 83)
● Augusta Vindelicorum
RHAETIA (15BC)
NORICUM (15BC)
Carnuntum ●
● Noreia
A L P S
Po
● Aquileia
Opitergium ●
● Vercellae
Rhône
Aquae Sextiae

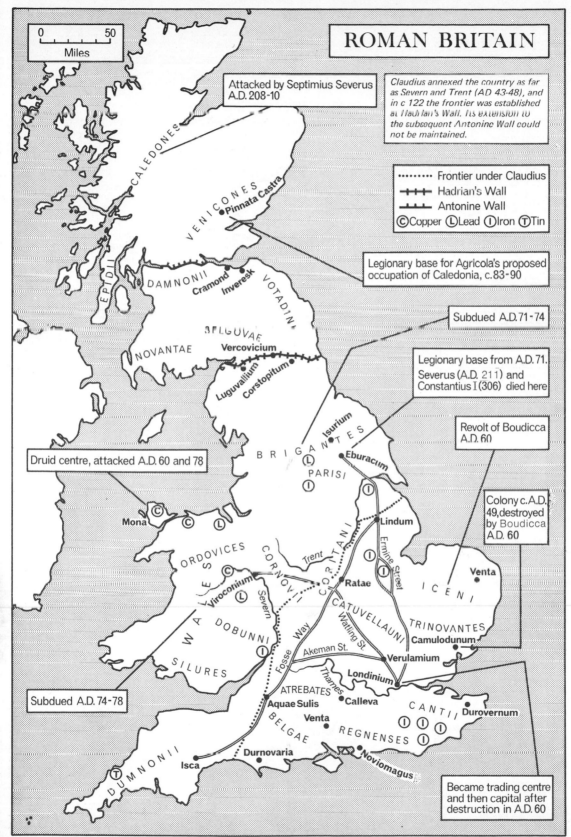

ROMAN BRITAIN

0 — 50
Miles

Claudius annexed the country as far
as Severn and Trent (AD 43-48), and
in c 122 the frontier was established
at Hadrian's Wall. Its extension to
the subsequent Antonine Wall could
not be maintained.

········· Frontier under Claudius
┼┼┼ Hadrian's Wall
⊥⊥⊥ Antonine Wall
©Copper ©Lead ①Iron ⊤Tin

Attacked by Septimius Severus
A.D. 208-10

Legionary base for Agricola's proposed
occupation of Caledonia, c.83-90

Subdued A.D. 71-74

Legionary base from A.D. 71.
Severus (A.D. 211) and
Constantius I (306) died here

Revolt of Boudicca
A.D. 60

Druid centre, attacked A.D. 60 and 78

Colony c.A.D.
49, destroyed
by Boudicca
A.D. 60

Subdued A.D. 74-78

Became trading centre
and then capital after
destruction in A.D. 60

CALEDONES
VENICONES
Pinnata Castra
EPIDII
DAMNONII
Cramond
Inveresk
VOTADINI
SELGOVAE
Vercovicium
NOVANTAE
Luguvallium
Corstopitum
BRIGANTES
Isurium
PARISI
Eburacum
Mona
ORDOVICES
CORNOVII
Viroconium
Lindum
CORITANI
Ratae
Venta
ICENI
WALES
DOBUNNI
Severn
Trent
CATUVELLAUNI
Watling St.
TRINOVANTES
SILURES
Akeman St.
Camulodunum
Fosse Way
Verulamium
Londinium
Thames
Ermine Street
ATREBATES
Calleva
CANTII
Durovernum
Aquae Sulis
Venta
BELGAE
REGNENSES
DUMNONII
Durnovaria
Isca
Noviomagus

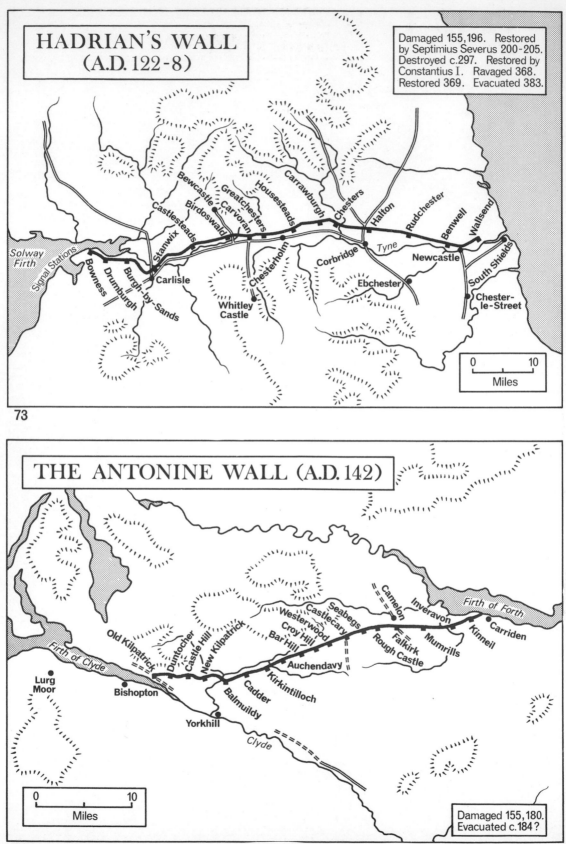

HADRIAN'S WALL
(A.D. 122-8)

Damaged 155, 196. Restored by Septimius Severus 200-205. Destroyed c.297. Restored by Constantius I. Ravaged 368. Restored 369. Evacuated 383.

Solway Firth

Signal Stations

Bowness
Drumburgh
Burgh-by-Sands
Carlisle
Stanwix
Castlesteads
Bewcastle
Birdoswald
Greatchesters
Carvoran
Housesteads
Carrawburgh
Chesters
Halton
Rudchester
Benwell
Wallsend
Newcastle
South Shields
Chesterholm
Chester-le-Street
Corbridge
Tyne
Ebchester
Whitley Castle

0   10
Miles

73

THE ANTONINE WALL (A.D. 142)

Firth of Forth

Old Kilpatrick
Duntocher
Castle Hill
New Kilpatrick
Bar Hill
Croy Hill
Westerwood
Castlecary
Seabegs
Camelon
Inveravon
Carriden
Kinneil
Mumrills
Falkirk
Rough Castle
Auchendavy
Kirkintilloch
Cadder
Balmuildy
Yorkhill
Bishopton
Lurg Moor

Firth of Clyde

Clyde

0   10
Miles

Damaged 155, 180. Evacuated c.184?

74

THE WORLD ACCORDING TO PTOLEMY, c. A.D. 150

The Geography of Claudius Ptolemaeus of Alexandria, including an atlas, showed awareness of the existence of China, but not of its shape.

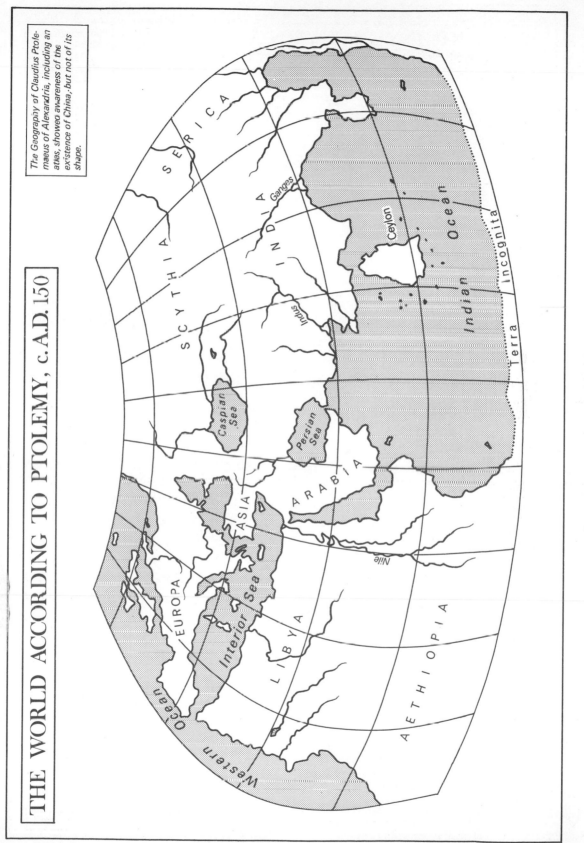

SERICA

SCYTHIA

INDIA

Ganges

Indus

Ceylon

Indian Ocean

Terra Incognita

Caspian Sea

Persian Sea

ARABIA

ASIA

EUROPA

Interior Sea

Nile

LIBYA

AETHIOPIA

Western Ocean

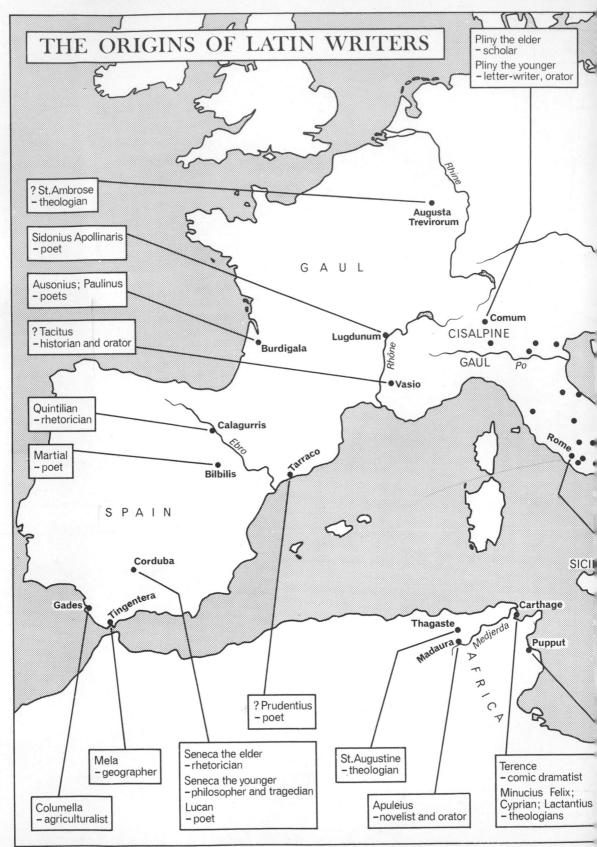

THE ORIGINS OF LATIN WRITERS

Pliny the elder
– scholar

Pliny the younger
– letter-writer, orator

? St. Ambrose
– theologian

Sidonius Apollinaris
– poet

Ausonius; Paulinus
– poets

? Tacitus
– historian and orator

Quintilian
– rhetorician

Martial
– poet

Mela
– geographer

Columella
– agriculturalist

? Prudentius
– poet

Seneca the elder
– rhetorician

Seneca the younger
– philosopher and tragedian

Lucan
– poet

St. Augustine
– theologian

Apuleius
– novelist and orator

Terence
– comic dramatist

Minucius Felix;
Cyprian; Lactantius
– theologians

GAUL

CISALPINE

GAUL

SPAIN

AFRICA

SICI

Augusta
Trevirorum

Comum

Lugdunum

Burdigala

Vasio

Calagurris

Bilbilis

Tarraco

Corduba

Rome

Gades

Tingentera

Thagaste

Madaura

Carthage

Pupput

Rhine

Rhône

Ebro

Po

Medjerda

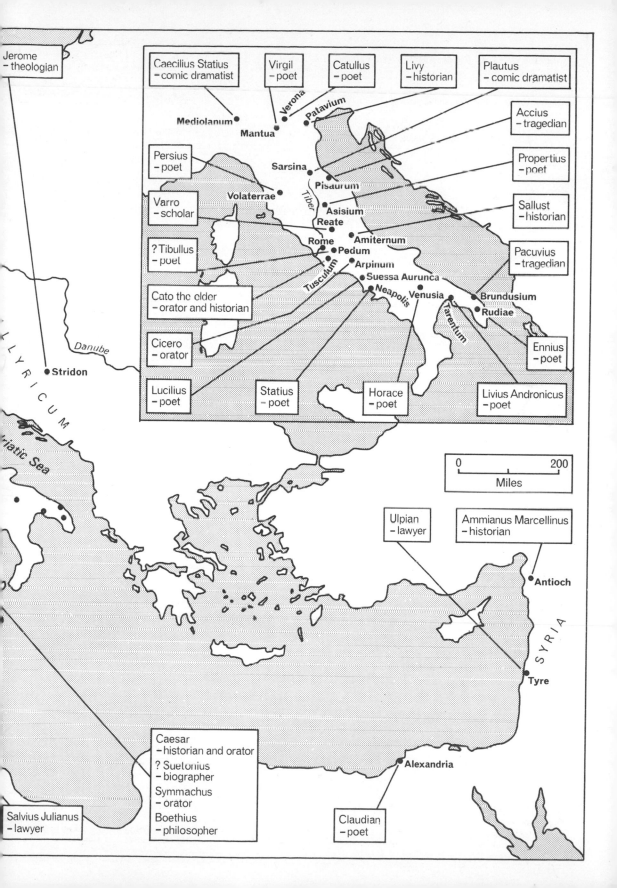

Jerome
– theologian

Caecilius Statius
– comic dramatist

Virgil
– poet

Catullus
– poet

Livy
– historian

Plautus
– comic dramatist

Accius
– tragedian

Persius
– poet

Propertius
– poet

Varro
– scholar

Sallust
– historian

? Tibullus
– poet

Pacuvius
– tragedian

Cato the elder
– orator and historian

Cicero
– orator

Ennius
– poet

Lucilius
– poet

Statius
– poet

Horace
– poet

Livius Andronicus
– poet

Ulpian
– lawyer

Ammianus Marcellinus
– historian

Salvius Julianus
– lawyer

Caesar
– historian and orator
? Suetonius
– biographer
Symmachus
– orator
Boethius
– philosopher

Claudian
– poet

Mediolanum

Verona

Patavium

Mantua

Sarsina

Pisaurum

Volaterrae

Asisium

Reate

Rome

Amiternum

Pedum

Arpinum

Tusculum

Suessa Aurunca

Neapolis

Venusia

Brundusium

Rudiae

Tarentum

Tiber

Stridon

Danube

ILLYRICUM

Adriatic Sea

Antioch

SYRIA

Tyre

Alexandria

0   200
Miles

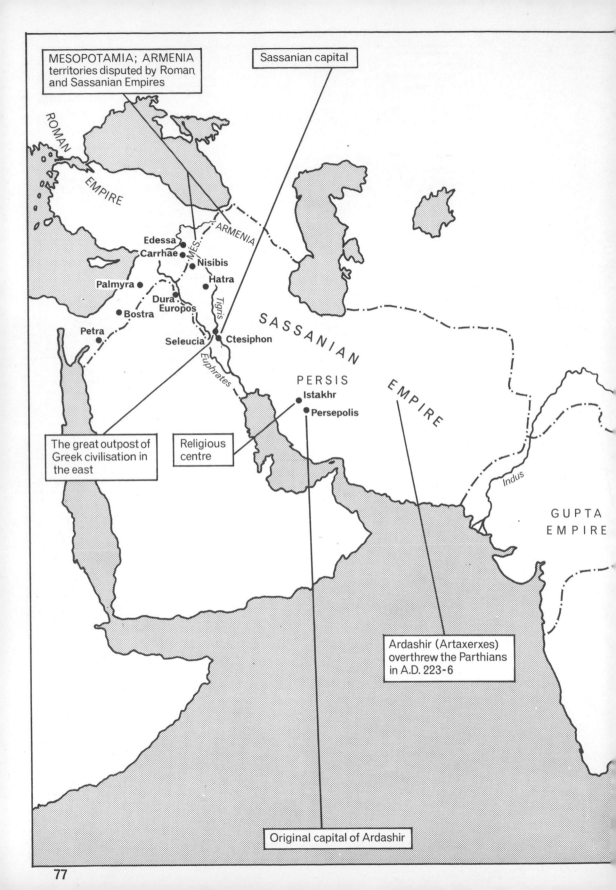

MESOPOTAMIA; ARMENIA
territories disputed by Roman
and Sassanian Empires

Sassanian capital

ROMAN

EMPIRE

ARMENIA

Edessa
Carrhae
MES.
Nisibis
Hatra
Palmyra
Dura
Europos
Bostra
Petra
Seleucia
Ctesiphon

Tigris

Euphrates

S A S S A N I A N

E M P I R E

PERSIS
Istakhr
Persepolis

The great outpost of
Greek civilisation in
the east

Religious
centre

Indus

GUPTA
EMPIRE

Ardashir (Artaxerxes)
overthrew the Parthians
in A.D. 223-6

Original capital of Ardashir

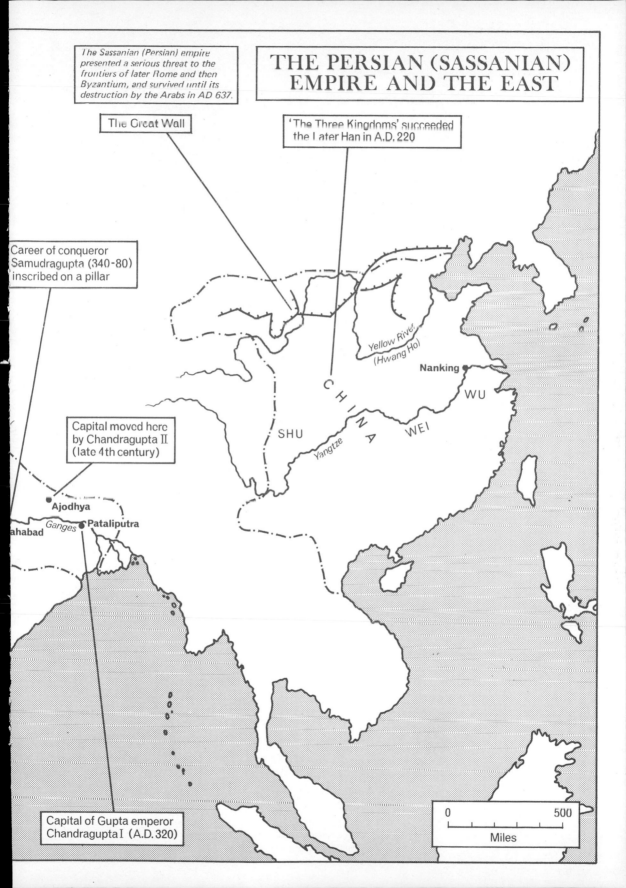

THE PERSIAN (SASSANIAN) EMPIRE AND THE EAST

The Sassanian (Persian) empire presented a serious threat to the frontiers of later Rome and then Byzantium, and survived until its destruction by the Arabs in AD 637.

The Great Wall

'The Three Kingdoms' succeeded the Later Han in A.D. 220

Career of conqueror Samudragupta (340-80) inscribed on a pillar

Capital moved here by Chandragupta II (late 4th century)

Yellow River (Hwang Ho)

Nanking

C H I N A

WU

SHU

WEI

Yangtze

Ajodhya

ahabad   Ganges   Pataliputra

Capital of Gupta emperor Chandragupta I (A.D. 320)

0   500

Miles

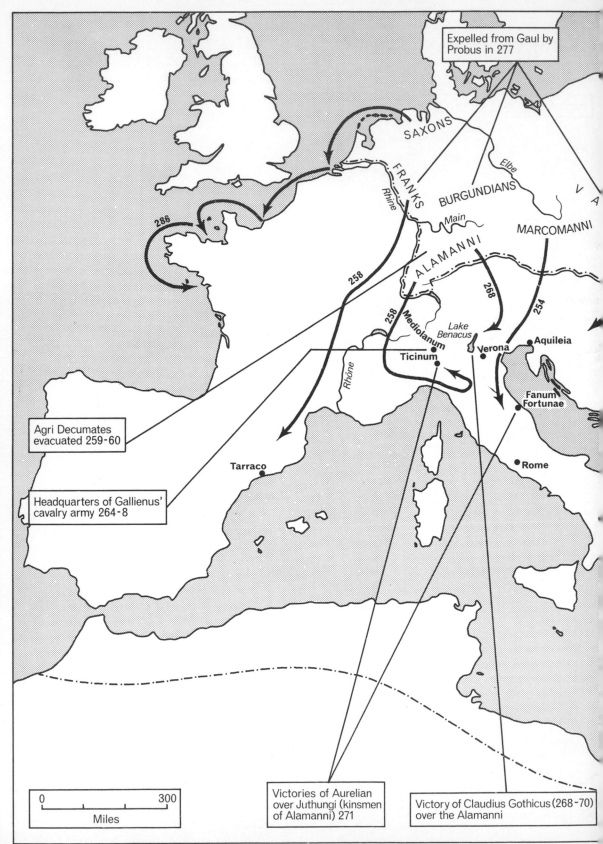

Expelled from Gaul by
Probus in 277

SAXONS

FRANKS

BURGUNDIANS

Rhine

Main

MARCOMANNI

Elbe

V A

A L A M A N N I

286

258

258

268

254

Mediolanum

Lake
Benacus

Aquileia

Verona

Ticinum

Rhône

Fanum
Fortunae

Agri Decumates
evacuated 259-60

Tarraco

Rome

Headquarters of Gallienus'
cavalry army 264-8

Victories of Aurelian
over Juthungi (kinsmen
of Alamanni) 271

Victory of Claudius Gothicus (268-70)
over the Alamanni

0   300

Miles

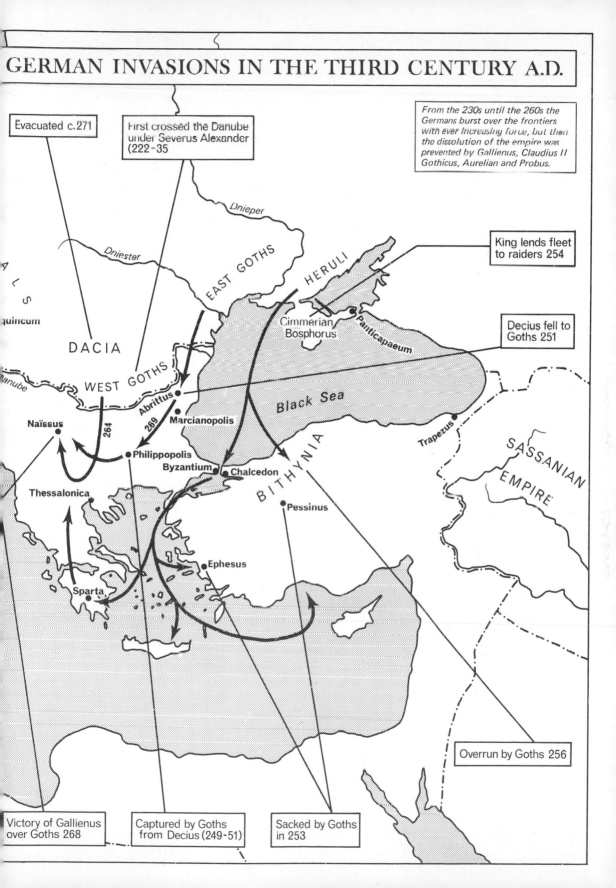

GERMAN INVASIONS IN THE THIRD CENTURY A.D.

Evacuated c.271

First crossed the Danube under Severus Alexander (222-35)

From the 230s until the 260s the Germans burst over the frontiers with ever increasing force, but then the dissolution of the empire was prevented by Gallienus, Claudius II Gothicus, Aurelian and Probus.

King lends fleet to raiders 254

Decius fell to Goths 251

Overrun by Goths 256

Victory of Gallienus over Goths 268

Captured by Goths from Decius (249-51)

Sacked by Goths in 253

Dnieper

Dniester

EAST GOTHS

HERULI

Cimmerian Bosphorus

Panticapaeum

quincum

DACIA

WEST GOTHS

Danube

Abrittus

264

269

Marcianopolis

Black Sea

Trapezus

SASSANIAN EMPIRE

Naïssus

Philippopolis

Byzantium

Chalcedon

BITHYNIA

Thessalonica

Pessinus

Ephesus

Sparta

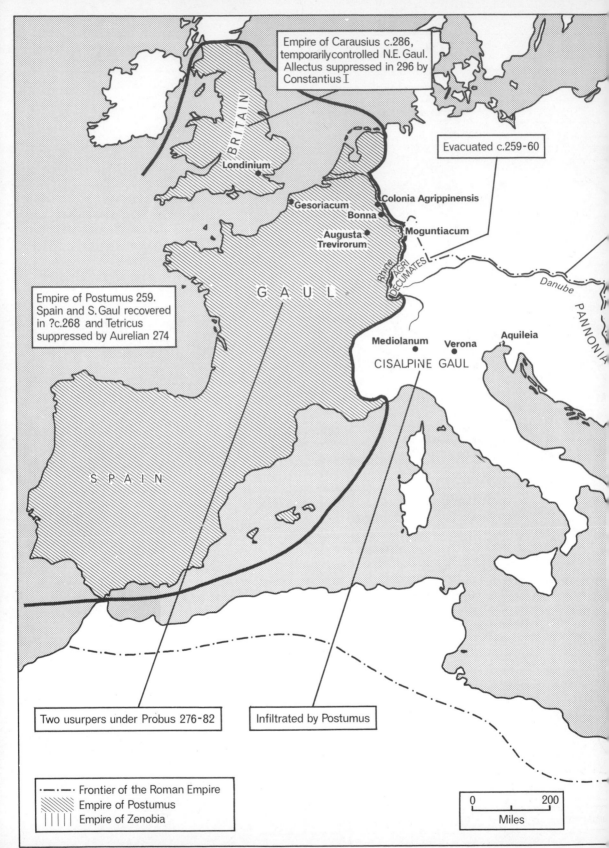

Empire of Carausius c.286, temporarily controlled N.E. Gaul. Allectus suppressed in 296 by Constantius I

Evacuated c.259-60

Empire of Postumus 259. Spain and S. Gaul recovered in ?c.268 and Tetricus suppressed by Aurelian 274

BRITAIN

Londinium

Gesoriacum

Colonia Agrippinensis

Bonna

Moguntiacum

Augusta Trevirorum

GAUL

AGRI DECUMATES

Danube

PANNONIA

Mediolanum

Verona

Aquileia

CISALPINE GAUL

SPAIN

Two usurpers under Probus 276-82

Infiltrated by Postumus

Frontier of the Roman Empire

Empire of Postumus

Empire of Zenobia

0   200

Miles

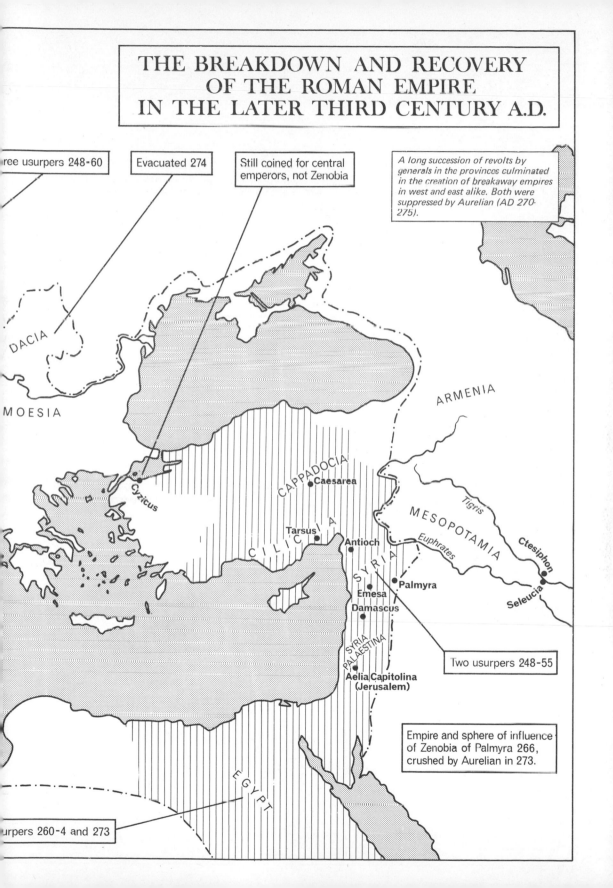

THE BREAKDOWN AND RECOVERY
OF THE ROMAN EMPIRE
IN THE LATER THIRD CENTURY A.D.

...ree usurpers 248-60

Evacuated 274

Still coined for central emperors, not Zenobia

A long succession of revolts by generals in the provinces culminated in the creation of breakaway empires in west and east alike. Both were suppressed by Aurelian (AD 270-275).

DACIA

MOESIA

ARMENIA

CAPPADOCIA

Caesarea

MESOPOTAMIA

Tigris

Cyzicus

Tarsus

C I L I C I A

Antioch

Euphrates

Ctesiphon

S Y R I A

Palmyra

Emesa

Seleucia

Damascus

SYRIA PALAESTINA

Two usurpers 248-55

Aelia Capitolina (Jerusalem)

Empire and sphere of influence of Zenobia of Palmyra 266, crushed by Aurelian in 273.

E G Y P T

...urpers 260-4 and 273

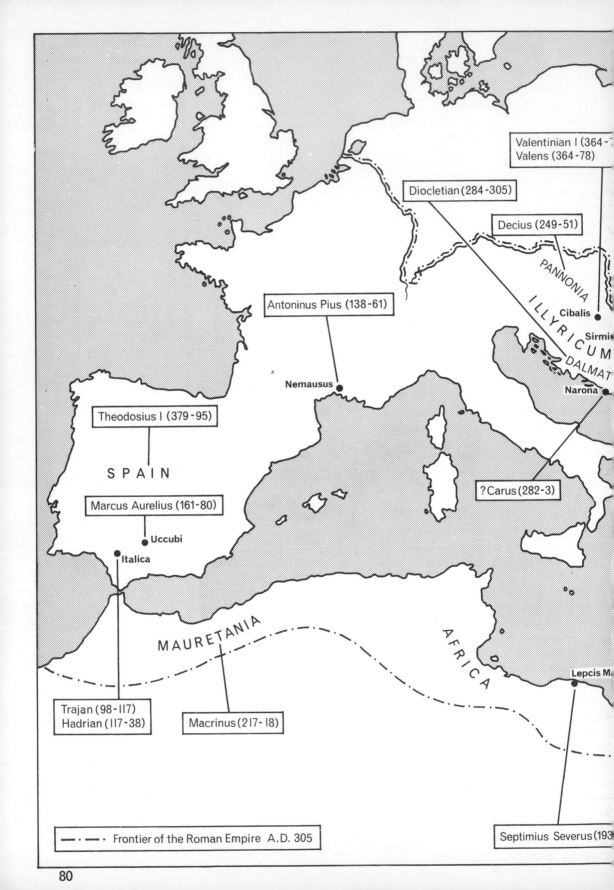

Valentinian I (364 -
Valens (364 -78)

Diocletian (284 -305)

Decius (249 -51)

PANNONIA

ILLYRICUM

Cibalis

Sirmi

DALMAT

Antoninus Pius (138 -61)

Narona

Nemausus

Theodosius I (379 -95)

SPAIN

?Carus (282 -3)

Marcus Aurelius (161 -80)

Uccubi

Italica

MAURETANIA

AFRICA

Trajan (98 -117)
Hadrian (117 -38)

Macrinus (217 - 18)

Lepcis Ma

—·— Frontier of the Roman Empire A.D. 305

Septimius Severus (193

80

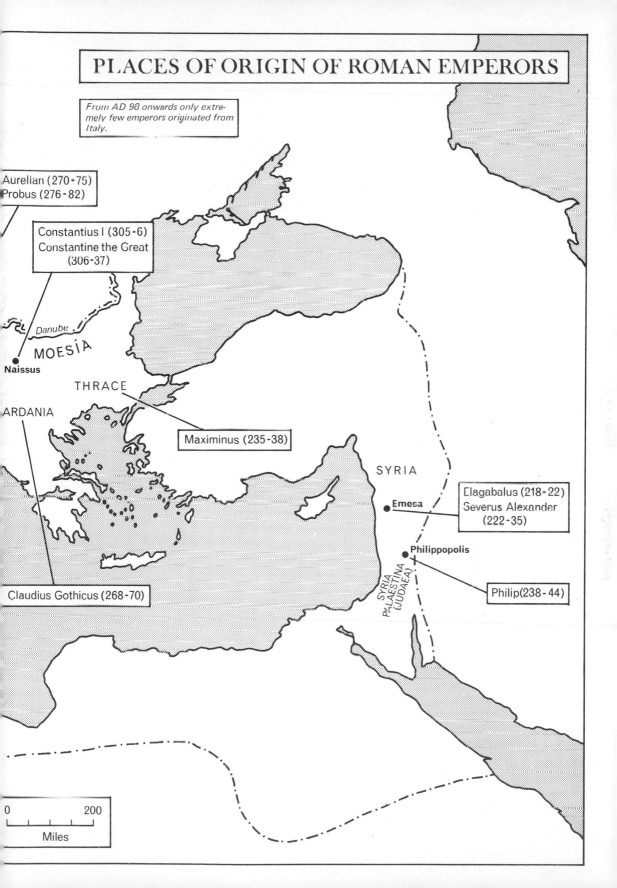

PLACES OF ORIGIN OF ROMAN EMPERORS

From AD 98 onwards only extremely few emperors originated from Italy.

Aurelian (270-75)
Probus (276-82)

Constantius I (305-6)
Constantine the Great
(306-37)

Danube

MOESIA

Naissus

THRACE

ARDANIA

Maximinus (235-38)

SYRIA

Elagabalus (218-22)
Severus Alexander
(222-35)

Emesa

Philippopolis

Claudius Gothicus (268-70)

SYRIA
PALAESTINA
(JUDAEA)

Philip (238-44)

0   200
Miles

GERMANIA

Colonia

Rhine

Regina

Aquincum

PANNONIA

Murs

Lutetia

Genabum

Vesontio

Alps

Tergeste

Ravenna

DALMAT

GAUL

Burdigala

Tolosa

Pyrenees

Massilia

Genua

ITALY

APULIA

CALA

Rome

CAMPANIA

SARDINIA

SPAIN

Corduba

Jews deported from
Rome by Tiberius
A.D. 14 - 37

Caralis

Panormus

SICILY

Gades

Carthage

Melita

Volubilis

Oea

Atlas   Mountains

S A H A R A

0				250

Miles

Areas of widespread Jewish settlement

Towns with large Jewish communities

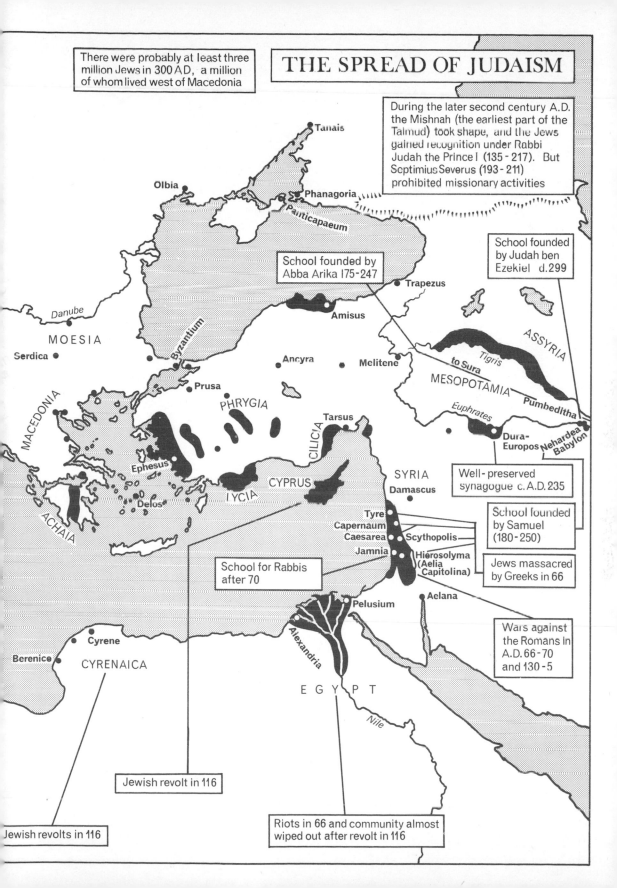

THE SPREAD OF JUDAISM

There were probably at least three million Jews in 300 AD, a million of whom lived west of Macedonia

During the later second century A.D. the Mishnah (the earliest part of the Talmud) took shape, and the Jews gained recognition under Rabbi Judah the Prince I (135 - 217). But Septimius Severus (193 - 211) prohibited missionary activities

School founded by Judah ben Ezekiel d.299

School founded by Abba Arika 175-247

Well-preserved synagogue c. A.D. 235

School founded by Samuel (180 - 250)

Jews massacred by Greeks in 66

School for Rabbis after 70

Wars against the Romans in A.D. 66 - 70 and 130 - 5

Jewish revolt in 116

Jewish revolts in 116

Riots in 66 and community almost wiped out after revolt in 116

Tanais

Olbia

Phanagoria

Panticapaeum

Trapezus

Amisus

Danube

MOESIA

Serdica

Byzantium

Ancyra

Melitene

to Sura

Tigris

ASSYRIA

MESOPOTAMIA

Pumbeditha

Prusa

PHRYGIA

Tarsus

Euphrates

Nehardea

Babylon

MACEDONIA

CILICIA

Dura-Europos

Ephesus

CYPRUS

SYRIA

Damascus

LYCIA

Delos

Tyre

Capernaum

Caesarea

Scythopolis

ACHAIA

Jamnia

Hierosolyma (Aelia Capitolina)

Aelana

Pelusium

Alexandria

Cyrene

Berenice

CYRENAICA

E G Y P T

Nile

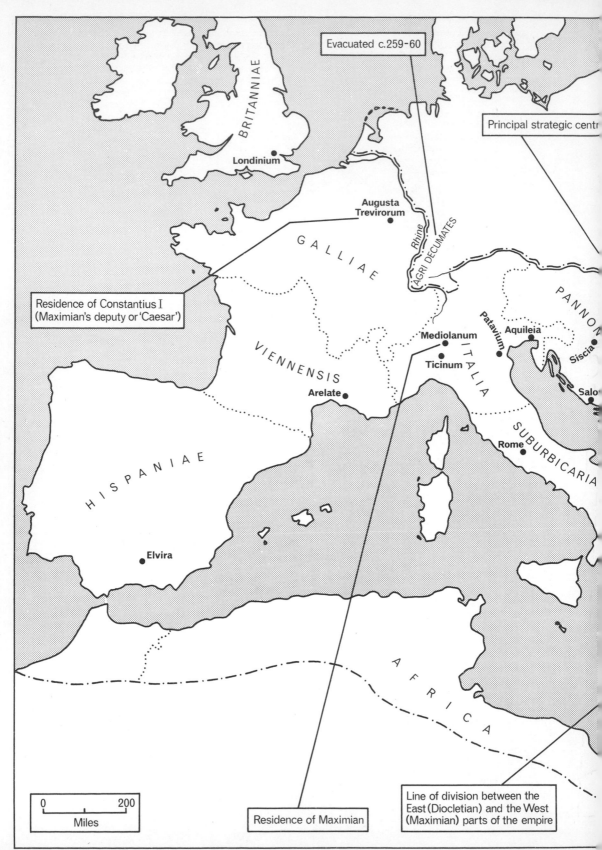

Evacuated c.259-60

Principal strategic centr[e]

Residence of Constantius I
(Maximian's deputy or 'Caesar')

BRITANNIAE

Londinium

Augusta
Trevirorum

GALLIAE

Rhine

AGRI DECUMATES

PANNON[IA]

VIENNENSIS

Mediolanum
Patavium
Aquileia
Siscia

Ticinum
ITALIA

Salo[na]

Arelate

SUBURBICARIA

Rome

HISPANIAE

Elvira

AFRICA

0   200
Miles

Residence of Maximian

Line of division between the
East (Diocletian) and the West
(Maximian) parts of the empire

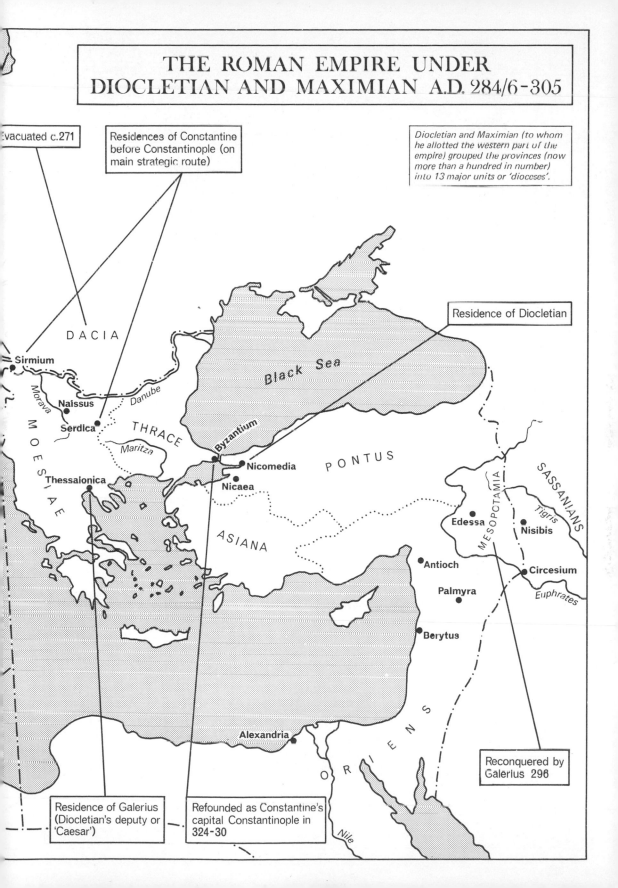

THE ROMAN EMPIRE UNDER DIOCLETIAN AND MAXIMIAN A.D. 284/6-305

Evacuated c.271

Residences of Constantine before Constantinople (on main strategic route)

Diocletian and Maximian (to whom he allotted the western part of the empire) grouped the provinces (now more than a hundred in number) into 13 major units or 'dioceses'.

Residence of Diocletian

DACIA

Black Sea

Sirmium

Morava

Naissus

Danube

Serdica

THRACE

Maritza

Byzantium

Nicomedia

PONTUS

MESOPOTAMIA

SASSANIANS

Tigris

M O E S I A E

Thessalonica

Nicaea

Edessa

Nisibis

ASIANA

Antioch

Circesium

Palmyra

Euphrates

Berytus

O R I E N S

Alexandria

Reconquered by Galerius 296

Residence of Galerius (Diocletian's deputy or 'Caesar')

Refounded as Constantine's capital Constantinople in 324-30

Nile

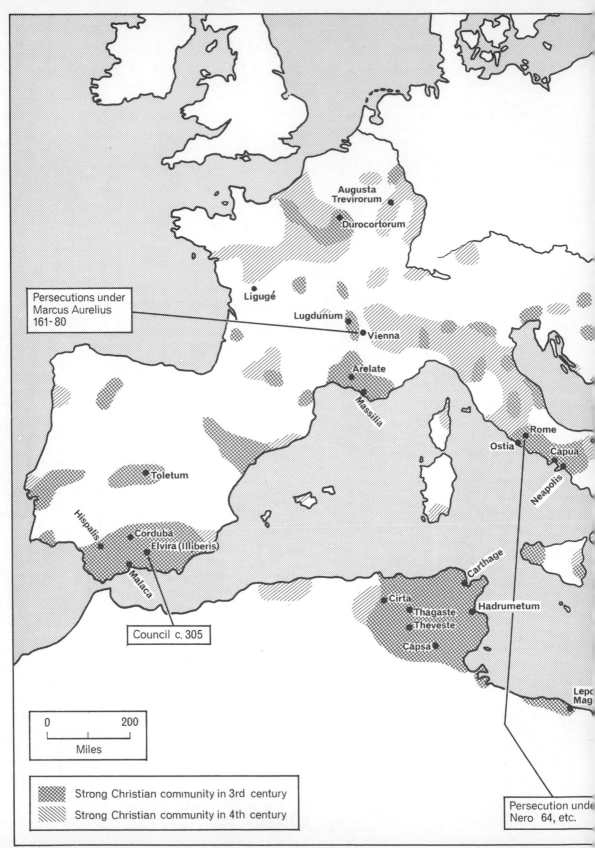

Augusta Trevirorum

Durocortorum

Persecutions under
Marcus Aurelius
161- 80

Ligugé

Lugdunum

Vienna

Arelate

Massilia

Rome

Ostia

Capua

Neapolis

Toletum

Hispalis

Corduba

Elvira (Illiberis)

Malaca

Council c. 305

Carthage

Cirta

Thagaste

Theveste

Hadrumetum

Capsa

**Lep[o]
Mag[**

Persecution und[e]
Nero 64, etc.

0   200

Miles

▨▨▨ Strong Christian community in 3rd century
⧄⧄⧄ Strong Christian community in 4th century

THE SPREAD OF CHRISTIANITY

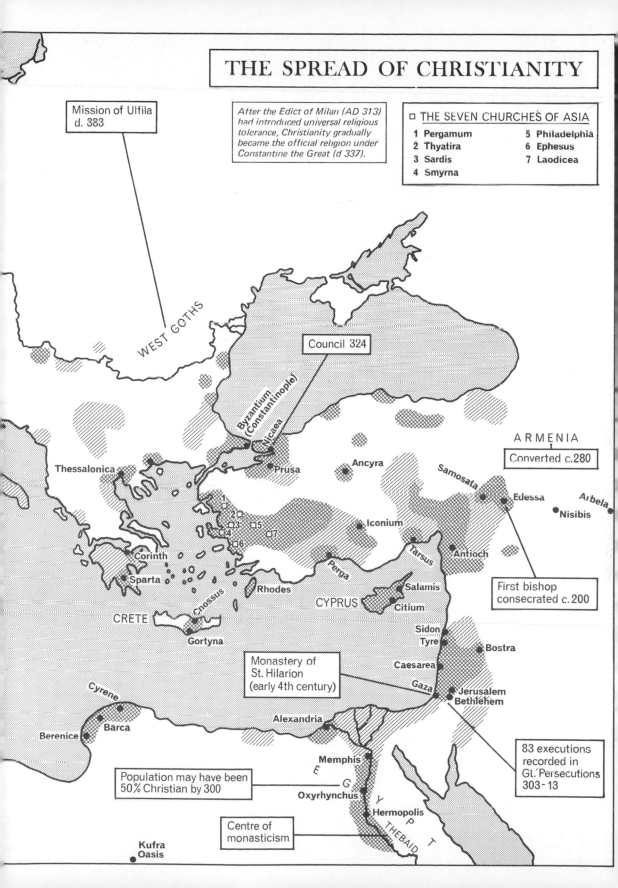

Mission of Ulfila
d. 383

*After the Edict of Milan (AD 313)
had introduced universal religious
tolerance, Christianity gradually
became the official religion under
Constantine the Great (d 337).*

THE SEVEN CHURCHES OF ASIA

1 Pergamum	**5** Philadelphia
2 Thyatira	**6** Ephesus
3 Sardis	**7** Laodicea
4 Smyrna	

WEST GOTHS

Council 324

Byzantium
(Constantinople)
Nicaea

ARMENIA
Converted c. 280

Thessalonica
Prusa
Ancyra
Samosata
Edessa
Arbela
Nisibis

2
3
4
5
7
6
Iconium
Tarsus
Antioch

Corinth
Sparta
Perga
Rhodes
CYPRUS
Salamis
Citium

First bishop
consecrated c. 200

Cnossus
CRETE
Gortyna

Sidon
Tyre
Bostra
Caesarea
Gaza
Jerusalem
Bethlehem

Monastery of
St. Hilarion
(early 4th century)

Cyrene
Barca
Berenice
Alexandria

83 executions
recorded in
Gt. Persecutions
303-13

Memphis
E
G
Oxyrhynchus
Y
P
T
Hermopolis
THEBAID

Population may have been
50% Christian by 300

Centre of
monasticism

Kufra
Oasis

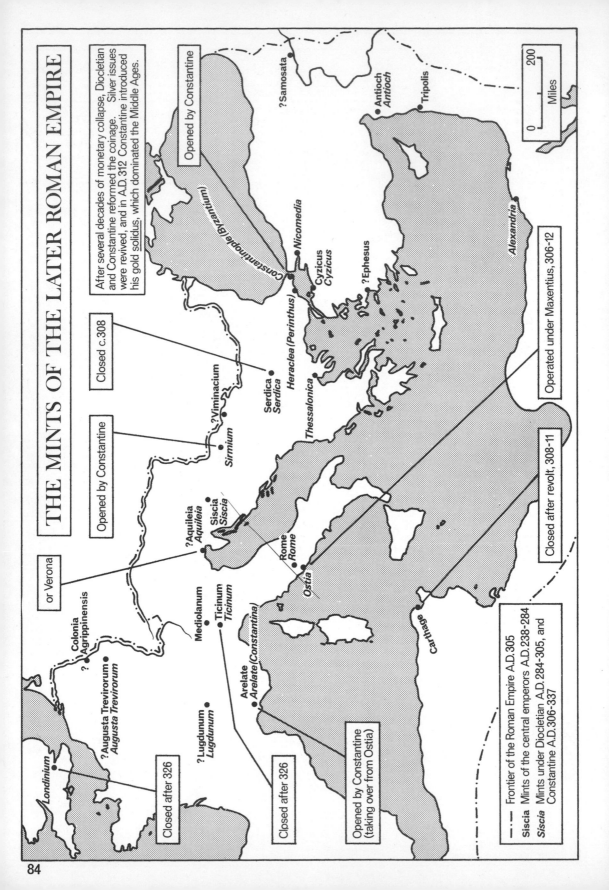

THE MINTS OF THE LATER ROMAN EMPIRE

After several decades of monetary collapse, Diocletian and Constantine reformed the coinage. Silver issues were revived, and in A.D. 312 Constantine introduced his gold solidus, which dominated the Middle Ages.

Opened by Constantine

Closed c.308

Opened by Constantine

or Verona

Closed after 326

Closed after 326

Opened by Constantine (taking over from Ostia)

Operated under Maxentius, 306-12

Closed after revolt, 308-11

?Samosata

Antioch
Antioch

Tripolis

Nicomedia

Constantinople (Byzantium)

Cyzicus
Cyzicus

?Ephesus

Alexandria

Heraclea (Perinthus)

Serdica
Serdica

Thessalonica

?Viminacium

Sirmium

?Aquileia
Aquileia

Siscia
Siscia

Rome
Rome

Ostia

Mediolanum

Ticinum
Ticinum

Arelate
Arelate (Constantina)

Carthage

Colonia
Agrippinensis

?

?Augusta Trevirorum
Augusta Trevirorum

?Lugdunum
Lugdunum

Londinium

0   200
Miles

— · —   Frontier of the Roman Empire A.D.305

Siscia   Mints of the central emperors A.D.238-284

Siscia   Mints under Diocletian A.D. 284-305, and
Constantine A.D.306-337

84

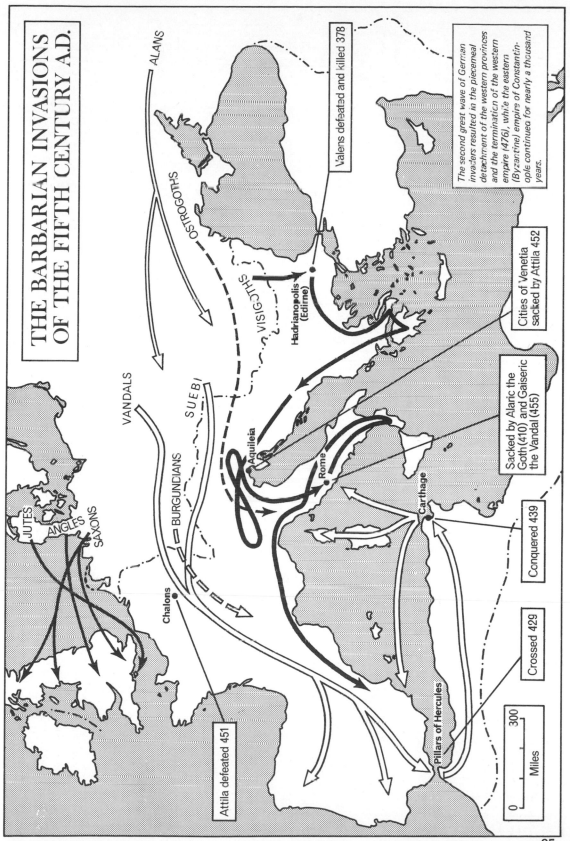

THE BARBARIAN INVASIONS
OF THE FIFTH CENTURY A.D.

ALANS

OSTROGOTHS

VISIGOTHS

Valens defeated and killed 378

Hadrianopolis
(Edirne)

The second great wave of German
invaders resulted in the piecemeal
detachment of the western provinces
and the termination of the western
empire (476), while the eastern
(Byzantine) empire of Constantinople continued for nearly a thousand
years.

Cities of Venetia
sacked by Attila 452

VANDALS

SUEBI

BURGUNDIANS

Aquileia

Rome

Carthage

Sacked by Alaric the
Goth (410) and Gaiseric
the Vandal (455)

Conquered 439

JUTES

ANGLES

SAXONS

Chalons

Attila defeated 451

Crossed 429

Pillars of Hercules

300

0

Miles

85

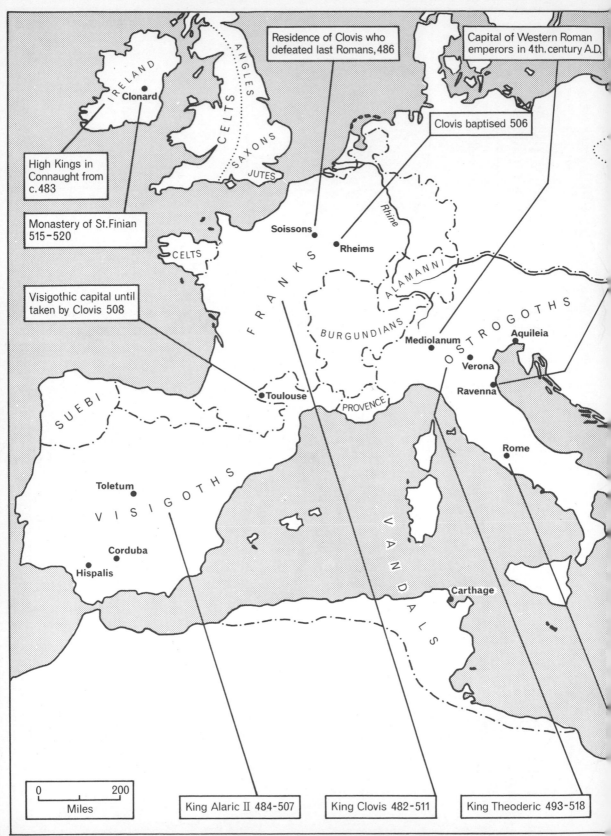

High Kings in
Connaught from
c. 483

Monastery of St. Finian
515–520

Visigothic capital until
taken by Clovis 508

Residence of Clovis who
defeated last Romans, 486

Clovis baptised 506

Capital of Western Roman
emperors in 4th. century A.D.

IRELAND

Clonard

ANGLES

SAXONS

JUTES

CELTS

CELTS

F R A N K S

Soissons

Rheims

Rhine

ALAMANNI

BURGUNDIANS

Mediolanum

O S T R O G O T H S

Aquileia

Verona

Ravenna

Toulouse

PROVENCE

Rome

S U E B I

Toletum

V I S I G O T H S

Corduba

Hispalis

V
A
N
D
A
L
S

Carthage

0   200
Miles

King Alaric II 484–507

King Clovis 482–511

King Theoderic 493–518

86

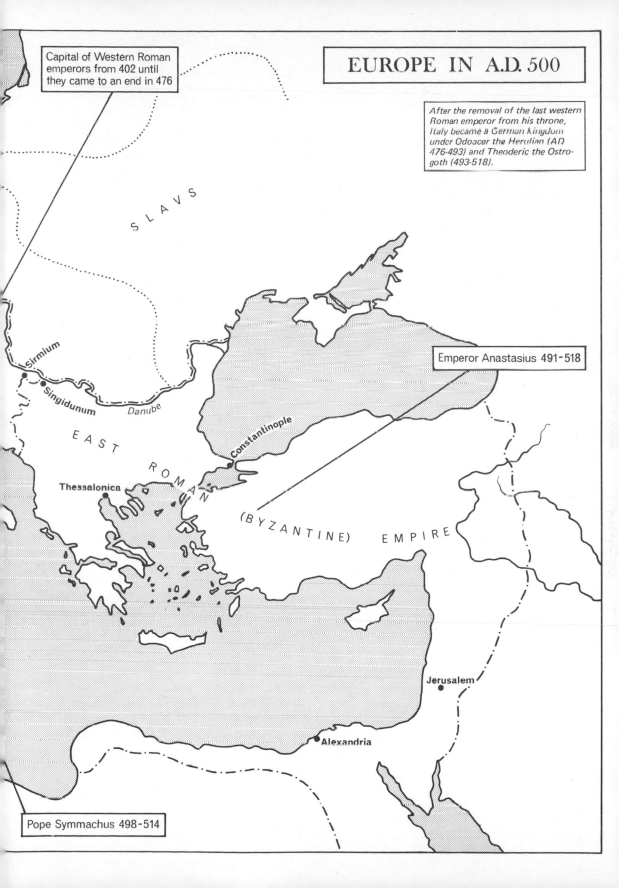

EUROPE IN A.D. 500

Capital of Western Roman emperors from 402 until they came to an end in 476

After the removal of the last western Roman emperor from his throne, Italy became a German kingdom under Odoacer the Herulian (AD 476-493) and Theoderic the Ostro-goth (493-518).

S L A V S

Sirmium

Singidunum

Danube

Emperor Anastasius 491-518

Constantinople

E A S T

R O M A N

Thessalonica

(B Y Z A N T I N E)   E M P I R E

Jerusalem

Alexandria

Pope Symmachus 498-514

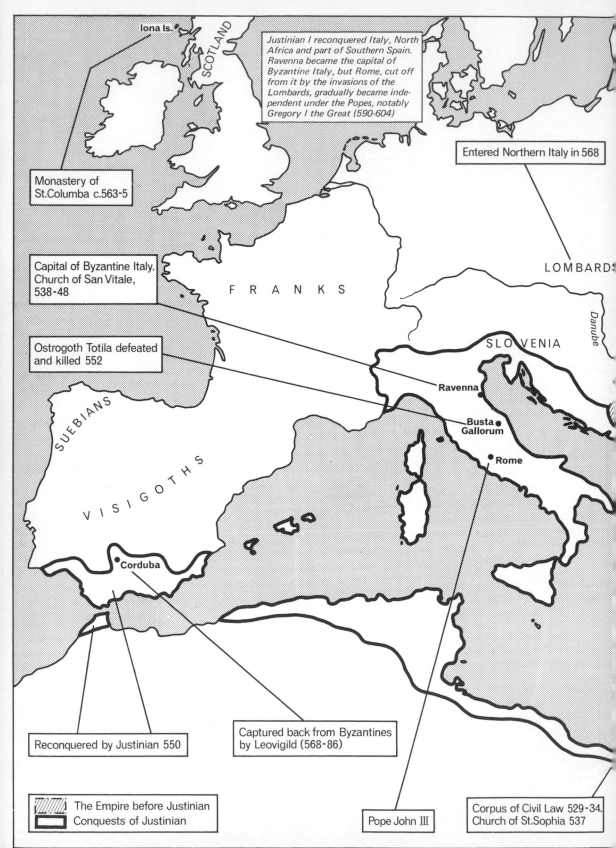

Iona Is.

SCOTLAND

Justinian I reconquered Italy, North Africa and part of Southern Spain. Ravenna became the capital of Byzantine Italy, but Rome, cut off from it by the invasions of the Lombards, gradually became independent under the Popes, notably Gregory I the Great (590-604)

Entered Northern Italy in 568

Monastery of St.Columba c.563-5

LOMBARDS

Capital of Byzantine Italy. Church of San Vitale, 538-48

F R A N K S

Danube

SLOVENIA

Ostrogoth Totila defeated and killed 552

Ravenna

SUEBIANS

Busta Gallorum

V I S I G O T H S

Rome

Corduba

Reconquered by Justinian 550

Captured back from Byzantines by Leovigild (568-86)

The Empire before Justinian
Conquests of Justinian

Pope John III

Corpus of Civil Law 529-34. Church of St.Sophia 537

87

THE BYZANTINE EMPIRE OF JUSTINIAN I
(A.D. 527-65)

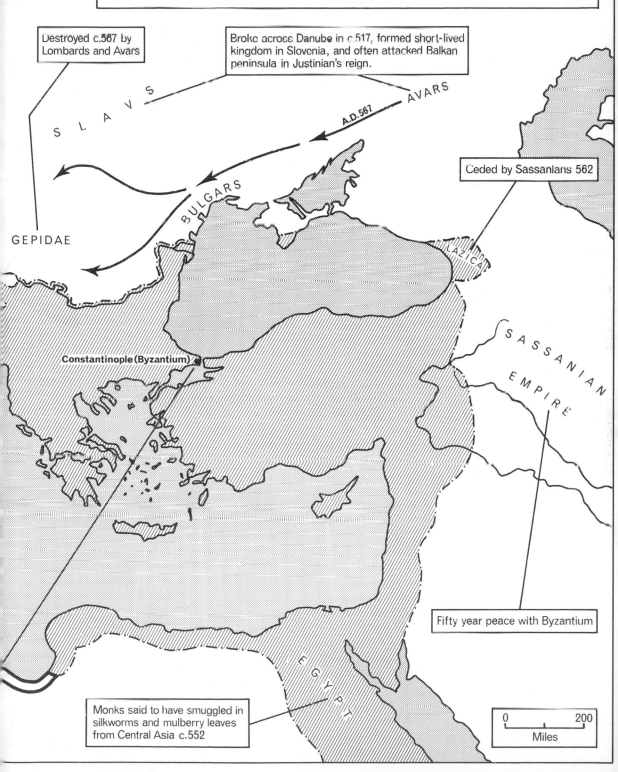

Destroyed c.567 by Lombards and Avars

Broke across Danube in c.517, formed short-lived kingdom in Slovenia, and often attacked Balkan peninsula in Justinian's reign.

SLAVS

AVARS

A.D. 567

Ceded by Sassanians 562

GEPIDAE

BULGARS

LAZICA

Constantinople (Byzantium)

SASSANIAN EMPIRE

Fifty year peace with Byzantium

EGYPT

Monks said to have smuggled in silkworms and mulberry leaves from Central Asia c.552

0   200
Miles

Index of Place Names[1]

Modern names are given in brackets

[1] I have sometimes sacrificed consistency of spelling to convenience and tradition.